THE MICROWAVE PLANNER

How To Adapt
Your Family Favourites

by
Annette Yates

PAPERFRONTS
ELLIOT RIGHT WAY BOOKS,
KINGSWOOD, SURREY, U.K.

Made and Printed in Great Britain by
Robert Hartnoll Ltd., Bodmin, Cornwall.

CONTENTS

Acknowledgements

I would like to record my sincere thanks to the following people and companies.

For her friendly advice and for the use of various microwave ovens: *Jay Oldknow, Toshiba (UK) Ltd, Toshiba House, Frimley Road, Frimley, Camberley, Surrey GU16 5JJ.*

For the use of a microwave oven: *Sharp Electronics, Sharp House, Thorp Road, Manchester M10 9BE.*

For the use of microwave cookware supplied by Lakeland Plastics, the mail order specialists: *Lakeland Plastics Ltd., Alexandra Buildings, Windermere, Cumbria, LA23 1BQ.*

For the use of an extensive range of 'MicroWare' and 'Freeze, Heat and Serve' microwave cooking utensils, manufactured by the Anchor Hocking Corporation: *The MicroWare Information Service, 271 High Street, Berkhamsted, Herts HP4 1AA.*

For their advice on power levels: *The Microwave Association, Pearl Assurance House, 128 Old Christchurch Road, Bournemouth BH1 1NL.*

For patiently deciphering and typing my scribbled pages: *Angela Sheldrake.*

This book is dedicated to my parents, John and Olive, who are 'always here' in Cefn Coed, near Merthyr Tydfil.

INTRODUCTION

If you are a microwave owner who still has to plan and make time to use the microwave oven, then this book has been specially written for you. It 'ties up the loose ends' of micro-wave cooking, helping you to convert your own everyday dishes – those family favourites you might prepare without thinking with the hob, grill or oven – for cooking in the microwave oven. It neither deals with the microwave or how it works, nor does it contain cooking charts for basic foodstuffs. All this and more has been covered in my earlier Paperfront books, 'Microwave Cooking Properly Explained' and 'Out of the Freezer into the Microwave'.

This book is the result of considerable research and is based on questions and suggestions put to me by numerous microwave owners (and prospective owners) in audiences all over the country. It is based also on surveys of everyday meals prepared by family members, friends, colleagues and audience members – meals prepared either regularly every week or at least once a month, as well as those prepared every now and again as a family treat. Hints and tips fill the pages from cover to cover, from alphabetical lists for everyday cooking, to meal plans and work plans which should help boost your confidence in using your oven and your time to the best advantage.

When we first learn to cook conventionally, whether it is at school, at home with parents, or when we set up our first home, all the basics have to be learned and many skills acquired. When we make mistakes we cannot always give up (after all, we all have to eat!). We keep trying other methods, other foods, and other recipes at least until we gain an acceptable repertoire. Tiresome as those early days may be, fortunately for our families and friends many of us go further and become excellent cooks. On the way to whatever standard of cooking we may each individually achieve, certain things become automatic, for example whether to use a saucepan or a frying pan, or use the grill.

The aim of this book is to show you when, *automatically,* it is to the microwave that you can turn. It is designed to help you reach the point where the microwave fits naturally into your system of cooking – whether it is for one person, a family, or for large numbers of people.

This book is for readers who think of their microwave ovens in terms of 'I should use it more often but have not got things quite together yet because I never get the time to understand it all...' etc. I do hope this book will become their helping hand.

Whether you are a new owner of a microwave oven or a more experienced user, Chapter 5, 'Using The Recipes', is essential reading.

Bon appetit.

Annette Yates

Note: Heart Pacemakers
Microwave ovens which are well maintained are perfectly safe. However, a few early types of cardiac pacemaker *may* be susceptible to interference when in close proximity to electro-magnetic fields such as those caused by microwave ovens and, incidentally, by some electric razors. If in doubt do not hesitate to seek medical advice.

1

MICROWAVE COOKWARE

Utensils which are suitable for use in microwave ovens allow microwaves to pass straight through them into the food. Since metal reflects microwaves, the food within it is not allowed to heat up. Microwave energy reflecting off a metal container could cause sparks which damage the microwave. Consequently metal and foil containers should not be used, neither should dishes or plates with silver or gold decorations – the decorations will cause sparking and will blacken. However, an exception to not using metal in the microwave oven is the use of foil to shield small areas of food (such as the wing tips on a chicken, for example) from over-cooking. Always follow your manufacturer's instructions carefully regarding the use of foil and never let it touch the oven walls.

So what can we use in the microwave? We can use most ordinary household materials: *ovenglass, glass ceramic, pottery, stoneware.* Utensils used for cooking must be able to withstand the heat created by the cooking food. For this reason paper, plastic, baskets, wood, waxed paper and card-board should be used for reheating for short periods only. Kitchen paper can be used to absorb moisture while microwaving.

There is a great variety of *microwave cookware* which has been specially designed for microwave cooking – in heat resistant plastic, glass and ceramic. When buying new cooking equipment, check that it is suitable for microwave cooking and if your model has a turntable make sure it fits on this. Some microwave containers are suitable for freezer use and for use in conventional ovens (up to a specific temperature) too. Check whether they are suitable for cooking foods with a high fat or sugar content, for example for Christmas pudding – not all plastic containers are suitable. Look out for useful starter sets of microwave cookware – an economical way of buying items of most use. A bumper pack of flexible plastic containers can be inexpensive. Use these to discover which shapes and sizes suit your cooking, before deciding to spend extra on the more sturdy types. An ideal sturdy set would include a large, round, shallow dish with a rack. Over this fits a high-domed, transparent lid which can double as a cooking container (you can see the contents too – an advantage, particularly with cake mixes). A cone completes the set, enabling the deep lid to be used as a ring mould.

Roasting bags make ideal cooking containers and can be used in the freezer too. They are light and easy to handle. Remember to pierce them or tie loosely to allow steam to escape. Ordinary plastic bags are not suitable for microwave cooking.

Cling film can be used to cover cooking food. Pierce it to allow steam to escape. See also page 30.

To test if a container is suitable for microwave use
Maybe you have some dishes in the cupboard and you are unsure whether they are suitable for microwave cooking. Try this test. Place the dish in the microwave oven and sit a cup or suitable container of cold water inside it (about 150ml/ ¼ pt). Microwave on HIGH for 1–2 minutes. The outer dish should remain cool while the water in the cup has become hot.

Try and save maximum effort and washing-up by cooking and serving (and perhaps freezing) in the same container. Mix and cook in the same dish. Flame-proof containers can be used for browning (meat for example) on the hob and then put into the microwave oven to finish cooking.

Note

Do not use containers which have been repaired with glue –
the glue will melt. Also a mixing bowl with rubber on its base
should not be put in a microwave oven – the rubber may
melt.

The shape of the container is important

Circular containers have the best shape since the microwaves
can penetrate equally to all sides of the food. The centre will
cook more slowly than the outer edges. Stirring helps
cooking.

A ring shape is very useful for foods which cannot be stirred
during cooking, e.g. cakes. The slow-cooking centre of a
circular dish has been removed.

Squares and rectangles receive extra microwave energy at
their corners. This causes over-cooking in foods which
cannot be stirred. In a rectangular dish there is also a slow-
cooking centre. Some manufacturers suggest covering the
short ends of the dish with foil to slow down the cooking of
food in these areas. Check with your instruction book for the
use of foil.

A *bowl* is the most useful container – it has no corners so the
microwaves enter the food evenly. It is particularly suitable
for foods which cannot be stirred and for sauces.

Containers with *sloping sides* have extra microwave energy
entering the food near the top edges and this area cooks first.
Even cooking is difficult in this type of container.

Microwave accessories

Over the years I have tried many microwave accessories.
There are five which I now find indispensable. You may wish
to add some of them to your cookware.

Browning dish

This has a special coating which heats up in the microwave
(see page 24 for details). A large dish with a lid is versatile – it
may be used as a casserole dish in which the meat and

vegetables can be browned first.

Microwave thermometer

This is particularly useful for successful cooking and defrosting of joints and whole poultry and is specially designed for use while the microwaves are switched on. Other thermometers should *only* be used while the microwave oven is not being operated because microwaves affect the mercury. Some microwave ovens have a thermometer or probe fitted inside the oven cavity. The microwaves switch off automatically, when the food has reached the required temperature.

Plate ring

For stacking plated meals for defrosting or reheating. One plate ring is sufficient – best (even) results are obtained if no more than two plates are defrosted and/or reheated at one time.

Roasting rack(s)

These are very useful for microwaving all types of food. Use them to lift dishes off the floor of the oven (I use them on a turntable too) so that microwaves have good access to the food from all angles. Food is cooked more evenly. Simply sit the food, dish or casserole on the rack. They are also useful for defrosting or cooking joints of meat. The meat is raised above its juices – to promote 'roasting' rather than 'stewing'.

Large jug

A large jug suitable for microwave use is an asset when making sauces, which must be allowed space to boil up during cooking. Even a small amount of sauce (particularly if it contains milk) boils up alarmingly.

2

DEFROSTING FOOD

The ability to defrost foods in minutes is one of the great advantages of the microwave oven. The need for advance planning of meals is not so urgent and it matters little if you forget to take food out of the freezer or unexpected guests turn up. A meal can still be ready for eating within the hour.

The DEFROST setting usually applies microwave energy to the frozen food in short bursts – a clever technique since a continuous burst of microwave energy would result in areas of melted food heating up while areas close by are still frozen. The DEFROST control ensures even defrosting – allowing heat from the melting parts to be conducted to the colder areas during the rest periods when the microwave energy is off. The chart on page 29 shows the percentage of the oven power used on this setting (30%–50%). In the unlikely event that your oven does not have a DEFROST control, defrosting can still be done, but it will take a little more effort and patience. Switch the microwave power on for 30–45 seconds then switch off for 1½ minutes. Continue this process until the food is defrosted.

Generally, defrosted foods require a *defrosting-standing time* when the temperature inside the food is allowed to even out and any remaining ice crystals to defrost normally. By allowing for this defrosting-standing time you will make sure that defrosting is even and that the food does not begin to heat up or cook at its edges. Some newer machines have an automatic defrost setting which works on a reducing basis, i.e. 70% power for 1 minute, dropping to 40% for 1 minute and 20% for a final minute. It is designed so that the machine's recommended defrost times effectively include a *defrosting-standing time* on certain foods. On those foods immediate cooking can follow. It may even be possible to programme the oven to change over from defrost to cook automatically on foods which allow this.

Some foods can be cooked from frozen. Vegetables are the best example. To ensure even defrosting and cooking, stir or shake them once or twice during microwaving.

Defrosting tips
Microwave-freezer containers save washing-up. Cook, freeze, defrost and reheat in the same container.

Freeze food in shallow blocks – they will defrost more quickly.

Defrost frozen food in a close-fitting dish. If the defrosted areas are allowed to spread over the base of a container they will attract more of the microwave energy and consequently over-heat. It is a good idea to line the container with a roasting bag, or foil before adding food which is to be frozen. This way the frozen block can be lifted out and packed away in the freezer. This is useful if you do not have a never-ending supply of microwave-freezer dishes. Remember to remove the foil before microwaving though.

Remove any lumps of ice which may be attached to the food – it will only slow down (and water down the food during) the defrosting process.

Separate large pieces of food such as sausages and chops as they defrost. This will encourage quicker, even thawing. Break up blocks of food (such as sauces and soups) as they soften.

Remove metal ties or foil containers before defrosting.

Open containers before defrosting to prevent them splitting or bursting open. The air inside will expand on heating. Pierce polythene bags.

Cover foods (except baked foods such as cakes, bread and pastries). This will hold in the heat and speed up the defrosting time.

Place cakes, bread and pastries on kitchen paper during defrosting, so excess moisture is soaked up.

Turn large pieces of food (such as meat joints) over, halfway through defrosting.

Remove any juices which come from joints and poultry as they defrost. They will only slow down the process by absorbing the microwave energy.

Finish defrosting large items – such as joints or whole poultry – by immersing in cold water during their defrosting-standing time.

Remove giblets from inside poultry as soon as possible.

Make sure poultry and meat are *completely* defrosted before cooking.

Use a microwave thermometer to tell you when the centre of a joint has defrosted.

Follow manufacturer's instructions for defrosting times until you are familiar with your oven. It is a good idea to note down times of quantities of food which you will regularly wish to defrost.

3

REHEATING FOOD

Microwave ovens are ideal for reheating cooked food. Its colour, flavour and texture are just like the freshly-cooked version. Individual portions are heated up speedily – a plated meal takes 3–4 minutes on HIGH. A family-sized casserole only takes 10 minutes on HIGH. Plated meals reheat very well with no drying out of the edges. Reheat two meals at a time by using a plate ring – they will take 5–7 minutes depending on their contents. Rotate the plates (in opposite directions) once during reheating.

When reheating food in the microwave, rules similar to those for cooking apply.

1. The *starting temperature* of the food will dictate its reheating time, e.g. food from the refrigerator will take longer than food at room temperature.

2. *Cover* or wrap foods during reheating to retain heat and moisture.

3. *Stir* sauces, soups, casseroles, milk puddings etc. to ensure even heating. *Turn* larger items such as chicken pieces, whole potatoes or corn-on-the-cob.

4. *Arrange* foods with care. (See page 22.) Foods on a plate should be arranged in one even layer, with thicker, denser items around the outer edge. For example, meat slices reheat very quickly and these are best placed in the centre of the plate. The underside of the plate will feel warm when the food is hot enough to serve.

5. *Under-estimate* reheating times if you are unsure. The

food can easily be put back into the microwave for a little longer and still takes minutes only. But overheated food over-cooks, dries up and spoils, and nothing will improve it.

6. Some foods *improve* with reheating. Slightly old bread freshens up on reheating. (Wrap it well in kitchen paper.) Casseroles improve their flavour on reheating – they have had time for all the flavours to develop and intermingle.

7. *Take care* when reheating pastry with a filling. While the pastry may feel warm, the inside will be much hotter. To avoid burning the mouth, allow a standing time for the temperature in the pie to equalise before serving.

8. *Use a thermometer* to check that meat joints and poultry are correctly heated to a temperature which is safe to eat. Either use a microwave thermometer (see page 80) during reheating or check the temperature regularly with a meat thermometer (but do not leave it in the microwave).

9. Foods which tend to *dry* on reheating benefit from reheating on a LOW or MEDIUM setting. Vegetables (without accompanying meat or sauce) and slices of sponge or Christmas pudding are good examples. Large pieces of food which cannot be stirred, e.g. lasagne, should be reheated on MEDIUM. Foods with plenty of moisture are safely reheated on HIGH.

Fibrous vegetables such as asparagus or broccoli are best reheated in a sauce.

4

ADAPTING YOUR OWN RECIPES FOR MICROWAVE COOKING

Cooking your own everyday familiar recipes in the microwave oven entails only slight variation in the preparation of ingredients and method of work.

Timing

The obvious difference between microwave cooking and conventional cooking is the timing. As a general rule, cook your favourite recipes for one quarter to one third of their usual cooking time. For example, a dish which takes 40 minutes to cook conventionally takes about 12 minutes to cook by microwaves. There will be foods which do not fit into this rule so it is a good idea to underestimate times and check the dish often when trying it for the first time. Undercooked food only requires a little extra time in the microwave to achieve the desired finish, but over-cooked food cannot be corrected. Compare the cooking time of a new recipe with a similar one in your manufacturer's instruction book as no one knows your particular model better than its manufacturer. Always be guided by this until you are confident of success. Use the ingredient with the longest cooking time as your guide to overall timing.

It is worth remembering that the following points will affect the timing:

1. *The type of food.* Foods containing moisture cook better than dry ones. The more moisture the food contains the longer it will take. Adding water to moist foods will also

lengthen the cooking time. Dense foods will take longer than porous foods: e.g. a piece of meat takes longer than the same quantity of minced meat. Extra cooking time on a lower power will be needed for tenderising tougher cuts of meat or for foods which need to absorb a lot of moisture, for example rice and dried foods. Foods which usually require gentle, slow cooking when prepared conventionally should be cooked on MEDIUM or 50% power. Variable power microwave ovens cope very well with this type of dish and the cooking time can still be half of that in a conventional oven. If your microwave oven does not have variable power control (see page 29) but has a DEFROST control this can be used for long, slow cooking.

2. *The quantity of food.* Two whole potatoes will take longer than one (though not twice the time) because the microwave energy has to be shared between the two items. If your microwave oven has a shelf, two layers of food can be cooked, but the cooking time will be longer. On the whole, food on the lower level tends to cook more slowly so foods with shorter cooking times should be positioned there. Generally though, avoid filling the microwave oven with food – with whole potatoes for example. It is quicker, and therefore more economical, to heat or cook small amounts.

3. *Its shape and thickness.* Perhaps the most important point to remember when preparing ingredients is to cut all meat and vegetables into even sizes as a regular shape will cook more evenly. It is a good idea therefore to bone and roll irregular-shaped joints of meat. Since thinner pieces of food cook faster than thick ones, where appropriate cut large pieces into smaller pieces to allow the microwaves to penetrate them faster. Thin areas of food may be shielded from microwaves with small pieces of kitchen foil. Check with your instruction book for the correct use of foil in your oven. Foil should not be allowed to touch the oven walls.

4. *The arrangement of the food.* If meat slices or pieces of fish are piled up in a cooking container they will cook unevenly. Make sure they are evenly distributed in the container. Arrange wedge-shaped foods with the tail end towards the centre (e.g. asparagus, small fish fillets). Tuck the tail ends of fish fillets under each other and overlap fish tails to produce a more even layer of food. When putting cooked meals on a plate for reheating later, make sure the arrangement is even (no high piles of potatoes for example).

5. *Its starting temperature.* Food at room temperature will cook in less time than food from the refrigerator or freezer. Cooking times given in this book are for foods at room temperature. Check that the food is ready after the minimum time – it can always be microwaved for a little longer. This avoids the risk of spoiling by over-cooking.

6. *The container used* particularly its shape. A regular shape with straight sides is best (see Chapter 1).

7. *The power level used.* Power levels enable you to adjust the amount of microwave energy entering the food. Use the chart on page 29 to guide your choice of power level.

Some microwave ovens incorporate sensors. These devices enable the oven to switch off when the food is cooked – by sensing the temperature, either on the food surface, or in the surrounding atmosphere. Other ovens may include computerised programs for specified weights of individual foods or made-up dishes. Check to see if the food or dish you are preparing is included in any of these. If not, then it is a good idea to use manual settings, following the advice given above.

Cooking-Standing Time
Always allow for a cooking-standing time. Food continues to cook after removal from the microwave oven, or when the energy is switched off. Heat is conducted from the hot outer

areas of the food to the cooler central areas. The cooking-standing time allows the cooking process to complete. The amount, size and density of food will dictate the cooking-standing time; larger, denser foods require longer times. Joints of meat, for instance, will go on producing heat and conducting it to the centre for 15 to 30 minutes after the microwave energy is switched off. As the chart on page 80 demonstrates, a joint will *increase* in temperature during the standing time. Other foods may need only a few minutes cooking-standing time, e.g. scrambled egg should be removed from the microwave oven when it is still slightly wet and runny.

With a little patience and practice, cooking times will become second nature and you will begin to gauge small differences automatically.

Turning and Stirring Food

Food cooked in a microwave oven needs to be turned and/or stirred to ensure even heating or cooking. Ovens with a turntable turn food automatically (remember to place the food off-centre where possible to ensure that the food receives microwaves evenly from all areas of the oven). Never position small items of food in a circle with one in the centre – the one in the centre will tend not to cook. Some microwave ovens have stirrers/paddles/antennae incorporated in their walls to encourage even heating and cooking. Foods such as soups, sauces and casseroles need to be stirred occasionally to encourage even cooking. Turn foods over (chops, chicken pieces, beefburgers, whole potatoes) once during cooking and swap foods such as meatballs from the outside of the dish to the centre.

Browning Food

Generally speaking, food cooked by microwaves does not brown. Since the heat which cooks the food is not directed onto its surface, it does not dry out, harden and brown. This 'drawback' seems to become less important as you get to know your oven, improve your methods, use attractive garnishes and even change your attitude to crisp and browned food. You will probably even prefer some foods without browned surfaces. Vegetables and cakes (with suitable decorations) are good examples of this.

Meat joints and whole poultry however will achieve a natural degree of browning, without assistance. Bacon rashers will brown and crisp too. Browning of meat and poultry improves its flavour (and probably its eye appeal too) and can be done before or after microwave cooking in the frying pan or under the grill. Some microwave ovens have browning elements or convection heating (the oven heats up conventionally as well as allowing microwaves to cook the food). Browning dishes or skillets may be purchased to suit your particular needs.

Browning dishes
These are designed specifically for microwave ovens. They are the only containers which are heated empty in the microwave. Their special coating absorbs the microwaves (on HIGH), reaching a temperature of up to 330°C/600°F. The food (particularly meat, sausages, eggs, fish, vegetables and toasted sandwiches) is placed on this hot surface where it sears and browns. Cooking is then completed by microwaves in the same dish. Though the handles become less hot than if they were in a conventional oven, always use oven gloves when using a browning utensil. Also, always protect your work surfaces with a heat resistant layer before placing the hot dish on them. Browning utensils are available in many shapes and sizes. Dishes with covers are more versatile. Griddles or skillets where the browning area sits inside a microwave plastic drip container are effective too.

Follow manufacturer's instructions carefully when using these containers. Never exceed the recommended pre-heating time.

Roasting bags
These are excellent for cooking larger joints of meat and whole poultry. Their natural browning is enhanced and a more even brown result is achieved. Remember to pierce the

bag to allow steam to escape during cooking. To promote browning, allow plenty of air between the meat and the bag and allow space for the bag to expand during cooking. It is a good idea to slit the bag in several places under the joint. Then place the meat on a rack in a tray. As the meat cooks, the juices drain away promoting better browning and preventing the meat from stewing. Instead of metal ties, use a piece of string or a strip of plastic cut from the end of the bag. Alternatively, split the bag open and cover the joint (which is placed on a rack), tucking the ends under.

Browning agents

These can be used to produce an appearance similar to conventionally cooked food. My feeling is that we should not be imitating conventional cooking but rather exploring and appreciating the microwave oven's potential. However, such browning agents are available to be sprinkled or spread onto food. Some of these flavour the food too, so they should be chosen with care, to complement the food.

Sauces such as soy, barbecue, brown, fruity, and Worcestershire can be used, as can soup and gravy mixes or stock cubes or granules. However each of these will alter the natural flavours and should be used carefully. Paprika mixed with melted butter gives good results when brushed over whole chicken. Glazes using honey, jams, chutneys, mustard, soy sauce or tomato purée make joints of beef and ham and poultry into 'special' dishes.

Toppings and colourings

Dishes such as casseroles and sauce-covered vegetables can be made more attractive in various ways. They can be browned under the grill before serving – but make sure the container is suitable. Alternatively, sprinkle toasted or fried breadcrumbs, grated cheese (particularly Parmesan) or crumbled bacon over the top. These will improve texture and flavour as well as the appearance of the dish.

Sweet dishes can be topped with brown sugar, chopped nuts, ground spices and so on. Cakes can include wholewheat flour, treacle, brown sugar, spices, chocolate, cocoa or coffee in their ingredients. Simple decorations such as a sprinkling of icing sugar will disguise a pale surface, as will the addition of icing with chopped nuts, grated chocolate, glacé cherries etc.

Healthy Eating with your Microwave

Current nutritional advice emphasises the need to ease up on our salt, fat and sugar intake, while increasing our consumption of foods which are rich in fibre. Whether you are on a strict diet – low calorie, low fat, salt free, etc. – or whether you are just generally aware of the need for a healthy diet, the microwave oven can be an asset.

Foods cooked in the microwave retain more of their authentic flavour than foods cooked conventionally. Not only do they cook quickly (another advantage in terms of nutrition) but also the majority of foods may be cooked using less (sometimes no) liquid. There is less evaporation so that flavours and nutrients are concentrated. If you are trying to cut down on salt intake for example, this flavour improvement makes up for the lack of salt. Remember too, that salt tends to dry and toughen the fibres of meat and vegetables, particularly when there is little cooking water to dilute it. In general it should be added *after* microwave cooking.

Since foods mainly cook in their own juices there is little need to add fat in microwave cooking. The true fresh flavours are retained and foods do not stick to the cooking utensil.

Individual portions are quick and easy in the microwave, involving less effort (and fewer cooking utensils) than conventional cooking. So if someone in your family is trying to cut down on calories, fat and sugar, it need not entail the preparation of a menu for one. In fact as time goes on you will probably discover that you have slowly moved over to a more healthy diet simply by increasing the number of dishes prepared in your microwave.

Checklist for Converting Recipes for Microwave Cooking

Finally, here is a checklist for cooking your favourite recipes in the microwave oven. Where it is appropriate, I have included the page number for more detailed information on this advice. You will also find handy checklists at the beginning of each section throughout the book.

For more details

1. Reduce the cooking time to about one third. — Page 20

2. Cook for the minimum time, rather than over-cook – check cooking progress often until you are confident. — Page 20

3. Check with a similar recipe in your instruction book. — Page 20

4. Cut ingredients into even sizes. — Page 21

5. Reduce the liquid in recipes such as soups and casseroles by about a quarter. If necessary more can be added during or after cooking. — Page 46 / Page 78

6. Use less or no fat. It is not needed to brown or to prevent sticking. Use a little, only to add flavour if wished. — Page 26

7. Use less salt and spicy seasonings. Adjust after cooking. — Page 26

8. Choose your power level. — Page 29

9. Arrange food evenly. — Page 22

10. Stir or cover foods which require stirring or covering during conventional cooking. — Page 30 / Page 23

11. Add delicate or quick-cooking ingredients towards the end of cooking.

12. Use quick-cooking or ready-cooked alternatives when a recipe asks for ingredients which would require such lengthy cooking times that other ingredients would over-cook, e.g. canned kidney beans and quick-cooking rice to go with chilli con carne.

13. When doubling recipe quantities, increase the cooking time by a quarter to one third.

14. When halving recipe quantities, decrease the cooking time by about one third.

5

USING THE RECIPES – VITAL TO ALL READERS

Cooking Times
Cooking times given in this book apply to a 600W–650W microwave oven. If your model differs in output, adjust the timings accordingly. Here is a guide:

600–700 W	500–600 W	400–500 W
30 sec.	35 sec.	40 sec.
1 min.	1 min. 10 sec.	1 min. 20 sec.
5 min.	5 min. 45 sec.	6 min. 45 sec.
10 min.	11 min. 30 sec.	13 min. 30 sec.
20 min.	23 min.	27 min.
30 min.	34 min. 30 sec.	40 min. 30 sec.

Variable Powers
I have recommended the ideal power level to use for your recipes. For ovens with one power level only, cooking times on HIGH are given. Where times on HIGH are *not* given, this means that the dish is suitable for the specified power level only.

Opposite is a guide to comparative power settings of variable power control microwave ovens, and their uses.

Conversion Tables
Stick to one type of measure. The following conversion tables give equivalent measures rounded slightly up or down for convenience.

10% WARM-HOLD approx. 65 watts	20-30% LOW/DEFROST 130-200 watts	40-50% MEDIUM/DEFROST 260-325 watts	60-70% ROAST 390-540 watts	80-90% REHEAT 520-580 watts	100% HIGH/FULL 650 watts
USE FOR:					
Keeping food warm. Rising yeast doughs. Softening butter and chocolate.	Defrosting slowly. Very slow simmering and baking. Developing flavour of sauces and casseroles.	Defrosting. Simmering and slow cooking of custards, stews, casseroles, pasta, rice.	Cooking critical ingredients, e.g. cheese, cream, eggs, mayonnaise. Defrosting whole poultry and meat over 2kg/4½ lbs. Pastry cases.	Reheating cooked foods. Cooking to retain extra moisture.	General cooking of fish, vegetables, fruits, tender cuts of meat, poultry and sauces without cream or eggs. Pre-heating browning dishes. Heating and boiling water, beverages etc.

Table compiled with the assistance of The Microwave Association
If the variable power settings on your microwave oven are indicated by numbers (e.g. 1–9) calculate
on the following basis:

9 = HIGH   3 = DEFROST
5 = MEDIUM   1 = LOW

Capacities

1 fl oz	25ml
2 fl oz	50ml
1/4 pt (5 fl oz)	150ml
1/2 pt (10 fl oz)	300ml
3/4 pt (15 fl oz)	400ml
1 pt (20 fl oz)	500–600ml

Spoon capacities

Spoon measures are level

1/4 tsp	half 2.5ml sp
1/2 tsp	2.5ml sp
1 tsp	5ml sp
2 tsp	10ml sp
1 tbsp	15ml sp

Weights

1 oz	25g	10 oz	275g
2 oz	50g	11 oz	300g
3 oz	75g	12 oz	350g
4 oz	100–125g	13 oz	375g
5 oz	150g	14 oz	400g
6 oz	175g	15 oz	425g
7 oz	200g	16 oz (1 lb)	450g
8 oz	225g	1 1/2 lb	700g
9 oz	250g	2 lb	900g

To Cover or Not To Cover – When you want to retain moisture, (e.g. casseroles, steamed sponge pudding), cover with a lid, pierced cling film or alternative polythene material. When retaining moisture would spoil the dish (e.g. crumble, bread) leave uncovered.

Cling Film – Recent research (as yet not fully substantiated) suggests that wrapping food in some types of cling film may be harmful. Cling film has been on sale for over 30 years with no adverse effects, but if you are worried about its safety, alternative polythene wrappings are available. In this book, cling film is used only to cover cooking food, e.g. over the top of a deep bowl where it does not touch the food. Always pierce cling film to allow steam to escape.

Automatic Temperature Probe or Sensor Device – Covering food may prevent such sensors from operating properly. Check with your instruction book to see if cling film should be used (or if food should be covered at all).

6

BREAKFASTS

BREAKFAST HINTS

Fresh Coffee
Fresh coffee prepared by the percolator or filter methods
need not be kept warm for hours. Simply reheat individual
cups in the microwave. One cup or mug takes $1\frac{1}{2}$–2 minutes
on HIGH.

Instant Coffee
Microwave a cup or mug of water on HIGH until just boiling
($1\frac{1}{2}$–2 minutes). Stir in the coffee powder or granules.

Tea
Place a tea bag in a cup and pour cold water over.
Microwave on HIGH for 2 minutes. Allow the tea to stand
until the desired strength is reached. Discard the tea bag.
Alternatively, microwave a cup or mug of water on HIGH
until just boiling ($1\frac{1}{2}$–2 minutes), add a tea bag and allow it
to stand until the required strength is reached.

Milk
Warm milk for drinking or for adding to cereals. Microwave
on HIGH in a cup or dish. $\frac{1}{4}$ pt/150ml milk takes about $1\frac{1}{2}$
minutes.

Orange and Grapefruit Juice
For frozen concentrated orange or grapefruit juice, remove
any metal from the carton and microwave on DEFROST. A

178ml/6¼ fl oz carton takes 2–3 minutes followed by a 3–5 minutes' standing time.

For freshly squeezed juices, warm whole oranges and grapefruits (or limes or lemons) on HIGH. This way they will yield more juice. Take care with the timing – over-heating will cause the fruit to burst.

1 orange takes about 15–30 seconds on HIGH
2 oranges take about 45 seconds on HIGH
3 oranges take about 1 minute on HIGH.

Croissants

Timing is crucial when heating croissants since an extra 5 seconds will ruin the result.

1 croissant takes 15 seconds on HIGH
2 croissants take 20–25 seconds on HIGH
3 croissants take 30 seconds on HIGH
4 croissants take 35–40 seconds on HIGH.

Toast

This cannot be made in the microwave oven.

Fried Bread

If you have a browning dish, pre-heat it on HIGH according to the manufacturer's instructions. Butter or oil the surface lightly and press each side of the bread with a spatula onto the browning dish for a few seconds.

An alternative to fried bread, which is very crispy, is made in the following way. Melt about 50g/2 oz butter in a small bowl on HIGH for about 1 minute. Brush this over one side of small bread slices. Arrange the slices, buttered side up on a roasting rack. Microwave on HIGH for 3–5 minutes, rearranging them halfway through the cooking time. They should feel dry and firm. As they cool the slices will crispen.

Bread

Use the microwave to freshen bread which is going stale. Microwave whole bread loaves, slices, or rolls on HIGH until heated through. Serve hot and they will taste freshly baked.

Butter

Soften butter for spreading. 4 oz/100g takes 5–10 seconds on HIGH.

Baked Beans

Always cover these in the microwave or they will splatter the oven walls. One portion takes about 1 minute on HIGH. (See recipe for Baked Beans on Toast on page 34.)

Eggs

Eggs can be scrambled, poached, baked and fried in the microwave. (See the individual methods on the following pages.) Timing is crucial for the last three methods (practice makes perfect) and the yolks of these eggs should always be pricked to prevent them from bursting open. Whole eggs in their shells can neither be boiled nor cooked in any way in the microwave. The build-up of steam inside the shell causes it to explode.

RECIPES FOR BREAKFASTS IN MINUTES

Bacon, Egg and Tomato

Method A

1. Cook the bacon under the grill so that the plates can be warmed at the same time.
2. Meanwhile microwave the tomato halves on HIGH until soft. Two halves will take about ½–¾ minute. Add ¼ minute for each extra tomato.
3. Break the eggs into individual buttered dishes or ramekins and pierce the yolks (to prevent them bursting).
4. Cover with saucers or absorbent paper. Best results are obtained by cooking on MEDIUM – the whites cook more evenly. Allow 1–1¼ minutes for 1 egg or 2 minutes for 2 eggs.
5. Allow the eggs to stand for a minute. Meanwhile reheat

the tomatoes and bacon on HIGH if necessary for ½–1 minute.

Method B

1. Cook the bacon on HIGH between two sheets of kitchen paper. Two rashers take about 1½–2 minutes on HIGH.
2. Meanwhile, heat the plates by immersing in a bowl of hot water.
3. Cook the tomatoes and eggs as in Method A.
4. Arrange the cooked bacon and tomatoes on the dried plates and reheat on HIGH for 1 minute if necessary while the eggs are standing.

Method C: using a browning dish

1. Pre-heat the browning dish on HIGH according to the manufacturer's instructions. Brush it lightly with cooking oil.
2. Press the rashers of bacon onto the dish for 10 seconds using a spatula, turn them over and press down for another 10 seconds.
3. Break the eggs into the dish, pierce the yolks, cover and microwave on HIGH with the bacon. (1½ minutes for 2 rashers of bacon and 2 eggs.)
4. Allow to stand for about 1 minute until the eggs are set.
5. Meanwhile, cook the tomato halves in a separate dish. Heat the plates in a bowl of hot water.

Baked Beans on Toast

Method A

1. Prepare toast using the grill (warming the plates at the same time) or toaster (warm the plates in a bowl of hot water).
2. Place a slice of hot buttered toast on a warm plate and spoon over 3 x 15ml sp (3 tbsp) baked beans.
3. Cover with an upturned plate and microwave on HIGH for 1–1½ minutes.

Method B

When preparing beans on toast for more than one person, I prefer to microwave the beans in a covered container on HIGH until warmed through. Then simply spoon them onto hot slices of buttered toast.

Eggs: Baked

1. Butter the inside of a suitable, small container or saucer.
2. Crack an egg into it and prick the yolk.
3. Cover with a saucer or absorbent paper.
4. Cook on HIGH: 1 egg takes 45 seconds – 1 minute
     2 eggs take about 1½ minutes
     3 eggs take about 2 minutes
     4 eggs take about 2½ minutes.

Eggs: Fried

The characteristic appearance and flavour of fried eggs can only be achieved when using a browning dish or skillet.

1. Pre-heat the dish according to the manufacturer's instructions. If you are cooking bacon on a browning dish or skillet as well, there will probably be sufficient fat in which to cook the egg (see Method C opposite). Otherwise lightly butter or oil the surface of the browning dish and crack an egg onto it. The heat will brown the base of the egg.
2. Prick the yolk and complete the cooking on HIGH for ½–1 minute.

Eggs: Poached

1. Microwave 150ml/¼ pt water on HIGH until it just boils. Add a pinch of salt and a dash of vinegar.
2. Break an egg into the water and prick its yolk.
3. Cover with a plate and microwave on HIGH for ½–1 minute.
4. Stand for 1–2 minutes before serving.

Eggs: Scrambled on Toast

Serves 1

	Met.	*Imp.*
Bread slice	1	1
Butter	To taste	To taste
Eggs	2	2
Milk	2 x 15 ml sp	2 tbsp
Butter	15g	½ oz
Salt and pepper		

Method
1. Toast the bread slice and keep it hot so that the eggs can be served immediately they are cooked. If using a grill, warm a plate at the same time. If using a toaster, warm a plate in a bowl of hot water. Butter the toast.
2. Beat together the eggs and milk in a suitable container. Add the 15g/½ oz of butter.
3. Microwave on HIGH for about 1½ minutes, stirring well after each 30 seconds. (3 eggs take about 2 minutes, 4 eggs take about 3 minutes.)
4. Allow the eggs to stand for 1 minute before seasoning with salt and pepper.
5. Serve on the hot toast.

Fish Fingers

Method A
1. Arrange the fish fingers (in a circle) on a suitable plate, and dot with butter.
2. Cook on HIGH: 2 take about 1½ minutes
             4 take about 2½ minutes.

Method B: using a browning dish
1. Pre-heat the browning dish/skillet according to the manufacturer's instructions. Spread with a little butter or oil.

2. Place the fish fingers on one half of the hot surface to brown quickly. Turn them over onto the other half.
3. Microwave on HIGH: 2 take ¾–1 minute
   4 take about 1½ minutes.

Kedgeree

Serves 4–6

	Met.	Imp.
Eggs	2	2
Smoked haddock	450g	1 lb
Long grain rice	225g	8 oz
Boiling water	400ml	¾ pt
Parsley, chopped	1 x 15ml sp	1 tbsp
Butter	25g	1 oz
Pepper		

Method
1. *Either* crack the eggs into suitable, small, buttered containers. Prick their yolks, cover and microwave on HIGH for 1½–2 minutes. Allow the eggs to cool before chopping them into small cubes.
   Or hard-boil the eggs in a pan on the hob and shell them and chop them when cold.
2. Microwave the haddock in a covered container on HIGH for 6 minutes and allow it to stand for 5 minutes.
3. Meanwhile put the rice into a suitable, deep container, pour the boiling water over, cover and cook on HIGH for 9 minutes. Allow it to stand for 5 minutes.
4. Flake the fish, discarding the skin and bones, and mix it with the rice, eggs, parsley, butter and seasoning to taste.
5. Reheat on HIGH for 3–4 minutes before serving.

Handy hint: Prepare this dish the day before for simple reheating in the morning.

Porridge

Serves 1

	Met.	*Imp.*
Quick-cook porridge oats	**50g**	**2 oz**
Water (check with packet instructions)	**150ml**	**¼ pt**
Salt	**Pinch**	**Pinch**

Method
1. Mix together the porridge and cold water in a suitable deep serving bowl.
2. Cover and cook on HIGH for about 3 minutes, stirring occasionally.
3. Add salt and allow to stand for 3 minutes before serving.

Time note: For each extra portion in the same container add 1–1½ minutes cooking time on HIGH.

7

SNACKS AND LUNCHES

Your microwave oven is invaluable for preparing quick snacks at any time of the day. Speedy lunches for one or for several people are no longer a chore.

HINTS FOR SNACKS AND LUNCHES

Bacon
This makes a quick and tasty snack, particularly in a sandwich. Microwave bacon rashers on HIGH between sheets of absorbent paper. Alternatively, use a browning dish or skillet. Cover the bacon with absorbent paper. The longer the cooking time the crisper the bacon becomes. Adjust the cooking times to suit personal preference. See page 34.

Frozen bacon rashers are quickly separated if microwaved on HIGH for 30-40 seconds and allowed to stand for a few minutes.

Beefburgers/Hamburgers

Your own recipes for beefburgers can be cooked in the microwave oven. The basic quantities for meatballs on page 57 may be prepared with beef, pork or lamb and shaped into your burgers.

Method A

Arrange the burgers in a circle on a roasting rack (or on absorbent paper) in a suitable, large, shallow dish. Cover with absorbent paper to prevent splashing and to soak up fat. 4 x 100g/4 oz burgers take about 6–8 minutes on HIGH. Turn over once during cooking.

Method B: using a browning dish

Pre-heat the dish/skillet according to the manufacturer's instructions and sear the burgers on both sides. Cover with absorbent paper and finish cooking them on HIGH. 4 x 100g/ 4 oz burgers take 5–6 minutes.

Frozen beefburgers are cooked from their frozen state, following methods A or B above.

> 1 takes about 2 minutes on HIGH
> 2 take about 4 minutes on HIGH
> 3 take about 5 minutes on HIGH
> 4 take about 6 minutes on HIGH.

Bread: Garlic or Herb

Soften butter in the microwave and mix with crushed garlic cloves, garlic powder or garlic purée, or chopped fresh or dried herbs. Spread this in a small French stick or Viennese loaf which has been sliced almost through to the base. Wrap the bread in absorbent paper and microwave on HIGH until the butter has melted in the bread.

Bread: Crispy Garlic or Herb Slices

Melt flavoured butter in the microwave and brush this over one side of quartered bread slices. Arrange (butter side up) on a roasting rack. Microwave on HIGH re-arranging them halfway through the cooking time, until they are dry and firm. The slices will crisp up as they cool.

Cheese

Cheese melts evenly in the microwave – on toast (see page 51) or simply on a plate to be served with fresh bread and pickle. Take care not to over-heat cheese, whether cooking by microwaves or conventionally, or it will become stringy and tough. Grate cheese to help it melt quickly and evenly.

Chips .

Ordinary chips *cannot* be deep-fried in the microwave. However, par-cooking them in the microwave speeds up cooking and produces crisper chips. Place the cut potatoes into a suitable container with a little water (60ml/4 tbsp to 450g/1 lb potatoes). Cover and cook on HIGH for about 5 minutes. The potatoes should be hot. Drain them, dry them and deep fry as normal.

Chips: oven

Oven chips can be cooked in the microwave though they will not be very crisp. Cook them from frozen.

Method A

The chips will not brown using this method.
Cook the chips in one even layer in a container between layers of absorbent paper. 225g/8 oz will take 6–7 minutes on HIGH. Allow a standing time of 2–3 minutes before serving.

Method B: using a browning dish

Pre-heat the browning dish/skillet on HIGH according to the manufacturer's instructions. Spread the frozen chips in one layer over the dish. Microwave uncovered on HIGH. 225g/8 oz take 6–7 minutes. Allow them to stand for 2–3 minutes before serving.

Croûtons

These make soups into filling meals. They are easily

prepared in the microwave. Thinly butter some bread slices, remove the crusts and cut the slices into small shapes. Spread these over a large, suitable plate and microwave uncovered on HIGH until they begin to crispen. 2 slices take about 2 minutes. They will go on crisping up as they cool.

To make flavoured croûtons, mix the butter (softened in the microwave) with crushed garlic, garlic purée or seasoning, finely chopped herbs, dried herbs or other seasoning.

You may prefer the crunchy texture of croûtons made without fat or flavour. If so, simply microwave plain bread shapes on HIGH until they are nearly dry and allow them to cool.

Eggs
Remember that eggs in their shells must neither be boiled nor cooked in any way in the microwave. The build-up of steam inside causes them to explode. Eggs can be baked, fried, poached and scrambled in the microwave oven and details can be found in the Breakfasts chapter (pages 35–36).

Omelettes
Microwave-cooked omelettes have a creamy texture. Melt a knob of butter in a wide, shallow dish and spread it over the base. Add the beaten eggs and microwave on HIGH. Lift the edges from the side of the dish after 1 minute so that the liquid area runs under the cooked portions. 2 eggs take 2–3 minutes on HIGH. Add any filling after the first minute.

Soufflé omelettes cook well in the microwave too. Blend the egg yolks with a little milk then fold in the beaten egg white. Follow the method for omelettes as above.

Pancakes
Pancakes cannot be cooked successfully in the microwave oven but they do reheat very well.

For savoury- or sweet-filled pancakes, prepare the fillings using the microwave while cooking the pancakes in a frying pan on the hob. I keep a stock of pre-cooked pancakes in the freezer for convenience – interleaved with greaseproof paper or non-stick paper. Fill the pancakes in advance and simply reheat in the microwave just before serving.

Pasta

Pasta should be microwaved in plenty of boiling water in a large, deep container. Use a long, flat dish for long shapes like spaghetti. Stirring in a little vegetable oil helps to prevent sticking. Place 225g/8 oz pasta in the container and pour over 1.2 litres/2 pints boiling water (from the kettle). Add salt and stir well. Cover and cook on HIGH for 7–9 minutes or until the pasta is almost cooked. Allow a standing time of 5 minutes before draining and serving. The pasta should still have a slight bite (*al dente*).

Pasta reheats well in the microwave too, either in a sauce or alone. Simply cover and microwave on HIGH for 2–4 minutes for the cooked quantity above. Stir gently once if possible. Adding a little melted butter or oil before reheating, prevents the pasta sticking. Allow a standing time of 1–2 minutes before serving.

Pâtés

Pâtés can be adapted for cooking in the microwave. When a recipe calls for liver or meat to be cooked (with or without fat) before mincing, do this in the microwave in a covered container on HIGH. Once the ingredients have been mixed together and shaped into a circular or loaf-shaped container, the pâté is best cooked on MEDIUM. Always cover the container during cooking to keep in the moisture. A 450g/1lb container of pâté takes 15–20 minutes on MEDIUM. Allow it to stand for 5 minutes after the first 10 minutes of cooking.

Cook kippers, mackerel and so on in the microwave before mixing with yoghurt, herbs and seasoning to make fish pâté.

Pizza

Though you may prefer to cook the base conventionally,

pizza dough can be cooked in the microwave. If using a bread dough, press it into greased plates, add a topping and cook uncovered on HIGH. Small individual pizzas take 5–6 minutes each; large ones take about 8 minutes. Turn them regularly if your oven does not have a turntable.

If using a scone dough, place on greased plates as above and cook uncovered on HIGH for 4–5½ minutes for each small pizza. A large pizza takes 6–7 minutes on HIGH.

If possible, use a browning dish to ensure that the pizza browns and crispens on its underside.

Pizza toppings with onions, tomatoes, mushrooms, herbs etc. can be prepared (in bulk for the freezer too) in the microwave.

Frozen pizzas are useful for speed. They can be heated from frozen on absorbent paper on a plate, on a roasting rack, or in a browning dish. Brush off excess ice crystals and microwave uncovered on HIGH until heated through (5–7 minutes for a 20–23cm/8–9 in pizza).

Potatoes in their Jackets

Always a favourite, whether eaten plain with butter, or with a dressing of yoghurt, sour cream, cheese or chilli sauce, the jacket potato is an excellent stand-by for a hot snack.

Prick washed, dried potatoes with a fork to prevent them from bursting. Stand them in a circle on absorbent paper. They should not touch each other or the oven walls. Cook, uncovered on HIGH turning halfway through cooking and taking out each potato as soon as it is cooked. Cooking times will depend on the size, type and age of potato, but here is a rough guide for potatoes weighing about 175g/6 oz:

> 1 takes 5–6 minutes on HIGH
> 2 take 8–10 minutes on HIGH
> 3 take 9–12 minutes on HIGH
> 4 take 10–15 minutes on HIGH.

Potatoes with Cheese: Split open a potato, add a knob of butter and top with grated cheese.

Potatoes with Tomato Sauce: Split open a potato, and pour in some tomato sauce (recipe on page 105).

Potatoes with Meat Sauce: Top a potato with the Savoury Minced Beef on page 48.

Potatoes with Chilli: Add chilli powder (to taste) to the Savoury Minced Beef recipe on page 48 and use this to top the potatoes.

Quiches

Best results are obtained if the pastry is cooked conventionally and the filling cooked in the microwave. (Instructions for microwave-cooking a pastry flan case appear on page 137.) Batch cooking pastry cases for the freezer is a good idea. Take one out when needed and complete the cooking in the microwave oven. Heating the egg mixture until slightly set before pouring into the pastry case helps the filling set quickly with less chance of making the pastry soggy.

Rarebits

Reduce the quantity of liquid slightly for microwave cooking. Stir the mixture once or twice during cooking.

Rice (for savoury dishes)

Rice grains are light, fluffy and separate when cooked by microwave. Wash the rice and place it in a suitable, deep container. Add a dash of cooking oil to help keep the rice grains separate. Pour on *boiling* water (a little more than 400ml/¾ pt to 225g/8 oz rice). Stir, cover and cook on HIGH. Allow a standing time of 5 minutes before stirring, seasoning and using.

225g/8 oz long grain rice takes 9 minutes on HIGH
225g/8 oz brown rice takes 15–20 minutes on HIGH

Sandwiches: 'Toasted'

Use a browning dish for 'toasted' sandwiches. Prepare the

sandwiches with the buttered sides out. Pre-heat the dish according to the manufacturer's instructions. Press the sandwich onto the dish and microwave on HIGH for 30 seconds. Turn the sandwich over onto a fresh (hot) area of the browning dish and microwave for a further 30 seconds on HIGH.

Sausages

Sausages cooked by microwaves do not look cooked – they do not have that characteristic brown appearance, and they easily over-cook. However, better results are obtained with a browning dish. Cooking times depend on their type and size, but the following is a rough guide for medium-sized sausages.

> 2 sausages take 3–4 minutes on HIGH
> 4 sausages take 5–6 minutes on HIGH
> 6 sausages take 9–10 minutes on HIGH.

Sausages cooked in a sauce or in a casserole are moist and tasty and the lack of crispy brown skins matters less.

Soufflés

These are not successful in the microwave. Soufflés need external heat in order to set a crust which traditionally holds the soft, light centre. A soufflé will rise in the microwave but will sink as soon as the energy is switched off.

Soups

Most soup recipes can be prepared in the microwave. Generally reduce the liquid quantity of ordinary recipes by about one quarter for cooking in the microwave oven as there is less evaporation. If the ingredients include dried vegetables or foods which absorb a great deal of moisture as they cook, you can always add extra liquid during cooking.

Use a container large enough to hold the soup without it boiling over, particularly those containing milk. Remember if your microwave does not possess a turntable to stir the soup occasionally to ensure even cooking.

Cook on HIGH unless the soup contains meat which needs tenderising – in which case cook on MEDIUM. Use the longest cooking ingredient as a guide to cooking times. Season after cooking – flavours will be more concentrated. Try making individual quantities of soup in a microwave-proof mug. Soften vegetables in a covered, deep container (with a little butter or cooking oil if liked). Add hot stock (boiling water from the kettle saves time and fuel if more than 550ml/1 pt is needed), other ingredients and flavourings. Cover and cook on HIGH for 15–20 minutes.

Dried Soups: Mix the powder with hot water (quantity given on the packet). Cook on HIGH for 4–6 minutes. Stand for 5–10 minutes.

Canned Soups: Dilute according to the instructions and heat on HIGH for 2–5 minutes.

Remember always to decant pre-packed cartons as the packaging may consist of metal or waxed paper which should not be put in a microwave.

Vegetables: dried
Dried vegetables, such as peas, re-hydrate well in the microwave. Place the vegetables in a suitable, large container. Cover with cold water according to the packet instructions. Microwave on HIGH for 8–10 minutes. Allow a standing time of 5 minutes before adding salt and sugar if liked.

RECIPES FOR SNACKS AND LUNCHES

Bacon, Lettuce and Tomato Sandwich

Serves 1

	Met.	Imp.
Streaky bacon rashers, rind removed	2	2
Bread slices	2	2

Bacon, Lettuce and Tomato Sandwich—contd.

Mayonnaise	1-2 x 15ml sp	1-2 tbsp
Lettuce leaves		
Tomato slices		

Method
1. Place the bacon rashers on a suitable plate and cover with absorbent paper.
2. Cook on HIGH for 1½-2 minutes (extra if you want the bacon really crisp). Allow it to stand for a minute. *Alternatively,* brown the bacon on a pre-heated browning dish.
3. Spread the bread slices with mayonnaise and arrange some lettuce leaves and sliced tomato on one piece.
4. Top with the crispy bacon and the other bread slice.

Handy hint: If you use a browning dish to cook the bacon you may prefer to 'toast' the sandwich in the browning dish too.

Baked Beans on Toast: See page 34.

Beef: Savoury Minced – (Bolognese)

Serves 4

	Met.	Imp.
Cooking oil	1 x 15ml sp	1 tbsp
Large onion, chopped	1	1
Streaky bacon, chopped	100g	4 oz
Carrots, chopped	2	2
Beef, minced	450g	1 lb
Beef stock, OR	150ml	¼ pt
Can tomatoes	397g	14 oz
Tomato purée	2 x 15ml sp	2 tbsp
Fresh chopped herbs, OR	2 x 5ml sp	2 tsp
dried herbs	1 x 5ml sp	1 tsp
Garlic cloves, crushed		
(optional)	1-2	1-2
Salt and pepper		

Method

1. Place the cooking oil, onion, bacon and carrots in a large, suitable container. Cover and cook on HIGH for 3 minutes, stirring once.
2. Stir in the minced beef, breaking it up with a fork. Cover and cook on HIGH for 5 minutes.
3. Drain off juices and skim off excess fat if wished. Return the meat juices to the mixture.
4. Mix in the stock or tomatoes along with the remaining ingredients.
5. Cover and cook on HIGH, stirring once or twice, for 15–20 minutes.

Handy hints: When cooking larger quantities for the freezer perhaps, increase the cooking time on HIGH. A mixture with 2.3kg/5 lb minced beef takes 35–45 minutes. Use this recipe as a base for Shepherd's/Cottage Pie (page 62) or Lasagne (page 55) or as a Bolognese Sauce (thicken with a little cornflour mixed with stock or red wine).

Cauliflower Cheese with Savoury Bread Rolls

Serves 4

	Met.	Imp.
Cauliflower florets	450g	1 lb
Water	4 x 15ml sp	4 tbsp
Butter or margarine	50g	2 oz
Flour	50g	2 oz
Milk	550ml	1 pt
Salt and pepper		
Cheese, grated	50g	2 oz
Bread rolls	4	4
Butter		
Crushed garlic, chopped herbs, dried herbs or lemon juice		

Method A

Cauliflower

1. Place the cauliflower florets and water in a large, suitable container.
2. Cover and cook on HIGH for 5–7 minutes. Allow a standing time of 5 minutes or more.

Sauce

1. Meanwhile prepare the sauce. Microwave the butter or margarine in a suitable jug on HIGH for about 1 minute.
2. When it has melted, stir in the flour then gradually add the milk, stirring continuously.
3. Cook uncovered on HIGH for 6–7 minutes, stirring frequently.
4. Season to taste and stir in the grated cheese.
5. Pour the sauce over the drained cauliflower.
6. Either reheat on HIGH for 2–3 minutes or brown under the grill.

Bread rolls

1. Mix together some butter (softened in the microwave) with crushed garlic, chopped fresh herbs, dried herbs or lemon juice.
2. Split the rolls and spread them with the flavoured butter.
3. Arrange the rolls in a circle on absorbent paper.
4. Microwave on HIGH for about 45 seconds or until the butter has melted in the bread.

Method B

1. Cook the cauliflower in a saucepan on the hob for 10–15 minutes.
2. Meanwhile, prepare the sauce in the microwave oven as in Method A.
3. While the sauce is standing, warm the bread rolls as in Method A.

Cheese on Toast

Serves 1

Toast a slice of bread, spread with butter and arrange cheese slices over it. Microwave on absorbent paper on HIGH for about 30 seconds or until the cheese bubbles.

Cheese Pudding

Serves 4

	Met.	*Imp.*
Breadcrumbs	225g	8 oz
Mature cheese, grated	225g	8 oz
Milk	550ml	1 pt
Butter	40g	1½ oz
Eggs, size 2	3	3
Mustard powder	pinch	pinch
Salt and pepper		

Method

1. Mix together the breadcrumbs and 175g/6 oz of the grated cheese and place them in a buttered 1¼ litre/2 pt soufflé dish.
2. Mix together the milk, butter, eggs, mustard powder, salt and pepper and microwave on HIGH until the butter melts.
3. Pour the mixture over the breadcrumbs.
4. Sprinkle over the remaining 50g/2 oz grated cheese. *Either* cover and cook on HIGH for 6–8 minutes, *or* cook on DEFROST for approximately 15–20 minutes, or until the pudding is set, in each case turning frequently if you do not have a turntable.

The pudding is cooked when a knife inserted in the centre comes out clean.

Eggs Florentine

Serves 4

	Met.	Imp.
White sauce(page 103)	550ml	1 pt
Spinach, washed	450g	1 lb
Salt and pepper		
Butter	knob	knob
Eggs, poached (page 35)	4	4

Method

1. Prepare the quantity of white sauce. While the sauce stands microwave the spinach with just the water clinging to its leaves, in a covered container on HIGH for about 5 minutes or until just tender. Drain and season it to taste and stir in a knob of butter.
2. Arrange the poached eggs on the bed of spinach.
3. Pour the white sauce over the eggs to coat them.
4. If necessary reheat the dish on HIGH for 2–3 minutes.

Fish Cakes

Serves 4

	Met.	Imp.
Potatoes, sliced	450g	1 lb
Fish fillets, such as cod, haddock etc.	450g	1 lb
Butter		
Egg, beaten	1	1
Salt and pepper		
Parsley or other fresh herbs, chopped	1–2 x 15ml sp	1–2 tbsp
Fresh breadcrumbs, toasted breadcrumbs, (page 133) or crushed cornflakes		

Method

1. Microwave the potato slices with a little water in a

covered container on HIGH for 5-8 minutes. Allow a standing time of 5 minutes.
2. Meanwhile microwave the fish, dotted with butter and covered, on HIGH for 3-5 minutes or until it begins to flake when tested with a fork.
3. Flake the fish, discarding any skin and bones. Mash the potatoes.
4. Mix together the potatoes and fish with the remaining ingredients.
5. Shape into cakes and coat with fresh breadcrumbs if cooking in a frying pan or under the grill. Coat with toasted breadcrumbs (see page 133) or crushed cornflakes if cooking by microwaves.
6. *Either* cook in a frying pan or under the grill, *or* place on a sheet of absorbent paper on a roasting rack, cover with more absorbent paper, and microwave on HIGH. Four fish cakes take 3-4 minutes. Allow them to stand for 2 minutes before serving.

Fish Florentine

Serves 4

	Met.	Imp.
White sauce, (page 103)	300ml	½ pt
Spinach	450g	1 lb
Salt and pepper		
Butter		
Fish fillets: cod, haddock, smoked haddock etc.	4	4

Method
1. Prepare the white sauce as described on page 103.
2. While the sauce stands, wash the spinach, shaking off the excess water. Cover and cook on HIGH for about 5 minutes or until just tender. Drain, season, and stir in a knob of butter if liked.
3. Place the fish in a suitable container, dot with butter,

cover and cook on HIGH for 3–6 minutes or until the fish begins to flake when tested with a fork.
4. Arrange the fish on top of the spinach and pour the white sauce over.
5. Reheat on HIGH if necessary for 2–3 minutes before serving.

Fish Pie

Serves 4

	Met.	Imp.
Potatoes, sliced	450g	1 lb
Fish: cod, haddock, coley	450g	1 lb
Butter		
White sauce, page 103	550ml	1 pt
Parsley, chopped	2 x 15ml sp	2 tbsp
Eggs, hard-boiled or baked in the microwave (see page 35)	2–4	2–4
Salt and pepper		
Toasted breadcrumbs (optional) page 133		

Method
1. Microwave the potato slices with a little water in a covered container on HIGH for 5–8 minutes. Allow a standing time of 5 minutes.
2. Meanwhile place the fish in a suitable container, dot with butter, cover and cook on HIGH for 3–6 minutes or until the fish begins to flake when tested with a fork.
3. Flake the fish, discarding any skin and bones.
4. Mix together the white sauce, parsley, chopped eggs and fish. Season to taste with salt and pepper.
5. Mash the potatoes and spread them over the fish mixture.
6. *Either* reheat the dish, uncovered, on HIGH for 3–5 minutes before serving. Top with toasted breadcrumbs

for an attractive finish. *Or* brown the surface under a hot
grill if the container is suitable.

Fish Pudding

Follow the recipe for Cheese Pudding on page 51. Replace
the cheese with 225–350g/8–12 oz fish (cod, smoked
haddock) which has been cooked in the microwave in a
covered container on HIGH for about 2–3 minutes or until the
fish flakes when tested with a fork. Flake the fish, discarding
any skin and bones. Add seasoning such as dill or parsley if
liked.

Lasagne

Serves 4–6

	Met.	*Imp.*
Lasagne sheets	175g	6 oz
Water, boiling	1 litre	1¾ pt
Cooking oil	1 x 15ml sp	1 tbsp
Savoury minced beef, page 48		
White sauce, page 103	550ml	1 pt
Cheese, grated	50g	2 oz

Method
1. Place the lasagne sheets in a wide, deep container and
   pour the boiling water and the cooking oil over. Cover
   and cook on HIGH for 5–8 minutes.
2. Allow it to stand for 2 minutes before draining and
   patting the lasagne dry with absorbent paper.
3. In a large container, arrange layers of the meat, lasagne
   and sauce, finishing with a layer of sauce.
4. Sprinkle over the grated cheese and microwave on
   MEDIUM for 10 minutes.
5. Brown under the grill if a brown, crispy surface is
   preferred and the container is suitable.

Macaroni Cheese

Serves 4

	Met.	*Imp.*
Macaroni	225g	8 oz
Water, boiling	900ml	1½ pt
Butter	40g	1½ oz
Flour	40g	1½ oz
Milk	400ml	¾ pt
Salt and pepper		
Mustard powder	½ x 5ml sp	½ tsp
Cheese, grated	50–100g	2–4 oz
Toasted breadcrumbs (optional) see page 133		

Method

1. *Either* cook the macaroni on the hob (according to packet instructions) while you prepare the sauce. *Or* place the macaroni in a suitable, deep container and pour over the boiling water. Cover and cook on HIGH for about 8 minutes. Allow it to stand while you prepare the sauce.
2. Melt the butter on HIGH, stir in the flour then gradually add the milk, stirring well.
3. Cook on HIGH for 5–6 minutes, stirring every 1½ minutes. Season to taste and add the mustard powder and grated cheese.
4. Drain the macaroni and stir this into the sauce.
5. *Either* reheat in a suitable container on HIGH for 2–3 minutes, and top with toasted breadcrumbs (optional, but gives an attractive finish), *or* brown the surface under a hot grill if the container is suitable.

Meat Loaf

Your favourite meat loaf recipes can be cooked in the microwave. Combine all the ingredients in the usual way and press the mixture into a suitable, greased loaf dish. Cover with greaseproof paper and microwave on HIGH. A loaf containing 700g/ 1½ lb raw minced meat will take 15–18 minutes. Use a microwave thermometer for accurate cooking.

Handy hints: A loaf shape tends to dry out at the short ends. Protecting these areas with a little foil helps the loaf cook more evenly – but check with your instruction book on the use of foil first. Alternatively, why not ring the changes and cook the loaf in a different shape. Individual meat loaves are interesting – arrange them in a circle in the microwave oven. A ring mould gives excellent results. Cooking is even since the loaf receives microwaves at its centre too.

Meatballs

Makes 20

	Met.	*Imp.*
Beef, lamb or pork, minced	450g	1 lb
Breadcrumbs	50g	2 oz
Tomato purée	1–2 x 15ml sp	1–2 tbsp
Onion, small, chopped	1	1
Mixed herbs, fresh or dried	to taste	to taste
Salt and pepper		
Egg, beaten	1	1

Method
1. Mix together all the ingredients and firm the mixture into balls.
2. Arrange them in one layer in a large, shallow container. Cover and microwave on HIGH for 10–15 minutes, moving the meatballs around the dish once or twice during cooking.
3. Allow a standing time of 3–5 minutes before serving.

Serving suggestion: These are delicious with tomato sauce (see page 105). Pour the hot sauce over the meatballs. Reheat if necessary for 3–5 minutes on HIGH.

Mushrooms with Garlic

Serves 4

	Met.	*Imp.*
Butter	25–50g	1–2 oz
Garlic cloves, crushed	1–2	1–2
Button mushrooms, wiped and trimmed	225g	8 oz
Salt and pepper		
Parsley, chopped	2 x 15ml sp	2 tbsp

Method

1. Place the butter and garlic into a suitable container. Cover and microwave on HIGH for 1 minute.
2. Stir in the mushrooms to coat them with butter.
3. Cover and cook on HIGH for 3–4 minutes, stirring once.
4. Season to taste and stir in the parsley just before serving.

Serving suggestion: Serve with toast, croûtons (see page 41) or crusty French bread.

Pasta with Tomato Sauce

Serves 4

	Met.	*Imp.*
Tomato Sauce, page 105		
Pasta shapes such as shells, twists, quills or bows	225–275g	8–10 oz
Water, boiling	1.1 litre	2 pt
Cooking oil	1 x 15ml sp	1 tbsp
Salt and pepper		

Method A

1. Prepare the sauce.
2. Place the pasta shapes in a suitable, deep container and pour the boiling water over. Add the cooking oil. Cover and cook on HIGH for 15–18 minutes (less if they are the quick-cooking type).
3. Allow a standing time of 2 minutes before draining.
4. Season to taste and pour the tomato sauce over.
5. Reheat on HIGH for 2–3 minutes before serving.

Method B

Prepare the pasta on the hob, following packet instructions while the tomato sauce is cooked in the microwave.

Serving hints: While the pasta and sauce are cooking, prepare a crunchy, green salad or some garlic bread (page 40) to serve with it.

Potatoes in their Jackets – see page 44.

Potato Pie

This is a substantial dish, particularly if cheese is added between the layers.

1. In a buttered soufflé dish arrange alternate layers of finely sliced potatoes (which have been rinsed and dried) and sliced onions. Season each layer with salt and pepper to taste.
2. Pour over sufficient milk (or cream and milk) to come almost to the top of the potatoes.
3. Dot with butter and microwave, covered, on HIGH for about 10 minutes for 450g/1 lb potatoes. Allow a standing time of 5–10 minutes.
4. Sprinkle with toasted breadcrumbs (see page 133) and/or grated cheese to improve its appearance before serving, *or* brown under a hot grill if the container is suitable.

Potato Salad

1. Microwave potatoes in their jackets on HIGH. See page 44 for a guide to cooking times.
2. Cool the potatoes before skinning them (if preferred) and cutting into cubes.
3. Mix with mayonnaise, chopped onion and seasonings to taste, until the potatoes are well-coated.

Potato Scones

Makes 8 scones

	Met.	*Imp.*
Self-raising flour	**100g**	4 oz
Salt	**pinch**	pinch
Butter	**25g**	1 oz
Potatoes, cooked and mashed	**100g**	4 oz
Milk		

Method
1. Sift together the flour and salt. Rub the butter into the flour until the mixture resembles fine breadcrumbs.
2. Mix in the cooked, mashed potato together with enough milk to make a consistency suitable for rolling out.
3. Roll out the mixture, on a lightly floured surface, to 1cm/½ in thick and cut into shapes.
4. *Either* arrange the scones in a circle on a sheet of non-stick or greased greaseproof paper. Microwave on HIGH for 3–5 minutes then allow them to cool on a wire rack. *Or* pre-heat a browning dish or griddle according to the manufacturer's instructions. Grease its surface lightly. Arrange the scones on the dish and microwave on HIGH for 3–4 minutes, turning over halfway through cooking. Cool them on a wire rack.

Quiche or Savoury Flan

Serves 4–6

	Met.	Imp.
Shortcrust pastry flan case	20cm	8 in
Eggs, size 3	3	3
Milk or milk and cream mixed	300ml	½ pt
Streaky bacon, chopped	4 rashers	4 rashers
Onion, small, chopped	1	1
Salt and pepper		
Cheese, grated	50g	2 oz

Method
1. *Either* cook the pastry case in the microwave following directions on page 137.
   Or bake the pastry case in the conventional way. This produces better results. Remember that the case may need transferring to a microwave-safe dish.
2. Mix together the remaining ingredients and pour them into the pastry case.
3. *Either* microwave, uncovered, on HIGH for 4–5 minutes, turning the flan halfway through cooking. Allow it to stand for 5 minutes. If the filling is not quite set, microwave on HIGH for a further ½–1 minute before allowing it to stand again.
   Or microwave on MEDIUM for about 15 minutes. The filling should finish setting if the flan is allowed to stand for 10–15 minutes.

You may find best results are obtained if you cook the filling mixture in the microwave (until it just begins to thicken) before pouring it into the pastry case. Finish cooking on HIGH or MEDIUM (as above).

Handy hint: Since better results are achieved with conventionally-cooked pastry cases, why not batch cook them for the freezer? Take one out when needed to fill and finish off in the microwave oven.

Rice: Savoury with Mushroom Sauce

Method A
Cook the rice in the microwave with some turmeric and/ or
herbs. Follow the guidelines on page 45. Meanwhile, prepare
the sauce using the method on page 103.

Method B
Prepare the sauce on the hob while the rice cooks,
unattended in the microwave. This will save time and give
you the opportunity to take your time and adjust seasonings
and flavourings to suit any simple or special occasion.

Shepherd's / Cottage Pie

Serves 4
1. Prepare a quantity of Savoury Minced Beef (page 48),
   adding your favourite herbs and flavourings.
2. Microwave sliced potatoes with a little water in a covered
   container on HIGH (450g/ 1 lb takes 6–8 minutes). Allow
   them to stand for 5 minutes before draining them and
   mashing them with salt, pepper, butter and a little milk.
3. Spread the potato over the mince in a suitable container.
4. Reheat on HIGH for 5–10 minutes. Brown the surface
   under a hot grill if liked, or sprinkle with toasted breadcrumbs or grated cheese for an attractive finish.

Soup: Bortsch

Serves 4–6

	Met.	Imp.
Beetroot, raw, grated	1 large	1 large
Carrot, grated	1	1
Onion, grated or chopped	1	1

Celery stick, finely chopped	1–2	1–2
Tomato purée	2 x 15ml sp	2 tbsp
Beef stock	550ml plus	1 pt plus
Butter	25g	1 oz
Lemon juice	2 x 15ml sp	2 tbsp
Bay leaf	1	1
Sugar (optional)	1 x 5ml sp	1 tsp
Soured cream		

Method
1. Mix together all the ingredients (except the cream) in a suitable, large container. Cover and cook on HIGH for 15–18 minutes, stirring two or three times during cooking.
2. Allow the soup to stand for 5 minutes before discarding the bay leaf. Add extra stock if needed.
3. Serve hot, garnished with a swirl of soured cream.

Serving suggestion: To serve the soup cold – omit the butter.

Soup: Tomato and Onion Cup

Serves 1

	Met.	*Imp.*
Cornflour	½ x 5ml sp	½ tsp
Chicken stock cube	½	½
Tomato, chopped	1	1
Spring onions, chopped	2–3	2–3
Salt and pepper		
Fresh herbs, chopped or dried herbs		
Milk or water		

Method
1. Place the cornflour and crumbled stock cube in a microwave-safe mug and stir in the tomato, onions,

seasoning and herbs. Half fill the mug with milk or water (not too full or the mug will overflow during cooking – you can always top up with milk or water after cooking).
2. Cover and cook on HIGH for about 3 minutes.
3. Allow the soup to stand for 3 minutes before serving.

Serving suggestion: Keep a supply of croûtons in a sealed container for occasions like this. See page 41 for details. This is good with crusty bread too.

Soup: Vegetable

Serves 4–6

	Met.	Imp.
Streaky bacon rashers, chopped	2	2
Onion, finely chopped	1 small	1 small
Leek, finely chopped	1	1
Celery sticks, finely chopped	2–3	2–3
Carrots, finely chopped	2–3	2–3
Potato, finely chopped	1 medium	1 medium
Cornflour	2 x 15ml sp	2 tbsp
Beef or chicken stock, boiling	1 litre	1¾ pt
Tomato purée	2 x 15ml sp	2 tbsp
Mixed dried herbs	½ x 5ml sp	½ tsp
Salt and pepper		

Method
1. Place the bacon and vegetables in a suitable, large container. Cover and cook on HIGH for 10 minutes, stirring once or twice during cooking.
2. Stir in the cornflour then gradually add the boiling stock (make up the stock from stock cubes and boiling water from the kettle if you like).

3. Add the remaining ingredients, cover and cook on HIGH for 10–15 minutes, stirring occasionally.
4. Allow the soup to stand for 5 minutes before adjusting the seasoning and adding extra stock or water if necessary.

Welsh Rarebit

Serves 1

	Met.	Imp.
Bread slice	1	1
Cheese grated	2–3 x 15ml sp	2–3 tbsp
Beer	2 x 5ml sp	2 tsp
Butter	knob	knob
Salt and pepper		
Mustard powder		

Method
1. Toast the bread slice.
2. Mix together the cheese, beer, butter, seasoning and mustard powder to taste.
3. Spread the mixture over the middle of the toast (it will spread quickly as it heats up) and place it on a sheet of absorbent paper.
4. Microwave, uncovered, on HIGH for 30 seconds until the cheese mixture is hot and bubbling.

8

MAIN MEALS

This section gives advice and hints on preparing a great variety of meat, fish and vegetable dishes which make up part or all of a substantial meal.

GETTING IT TOGETHER

A main meal provides an occasion when all your planning, preparation and co-ordination culminate in a delicious spread. It seems appropriate therefore, at this stage in the book, to talk about planning, preparation and co-ordination. Together with making the best use of your microwave alongside your other cooking appliances, the prospect can sound daunting. You may ask yourself how you can possibly 'get it together' and serve the meal on time. Perhaps my most important piece of advice would be to start slowly and advance gently. We all know that 'practice makes perfect' and that it takes a while to do so. Begin by preparing one or two simple items of a meal in the microwave – the vegetables perhaps. Then go on to simple recipes – basic ones from your instruction book which have been designed specifically for your microwave oven. As your confidence grows, you will want to cook your own recipes in the microwave. Pages 20–27 give numerous hints on adapting your own recipes for microwave cooking.

Ironically perhaps, you will not save time by attempting to cook *everything* in the microwave. So when time is short, prepare one dish in the microwave while cooking another on the hob, and so on. Meanwhile, here are some ideas for getting together three simple meals, a roast dinner or Sunday lunch, and, the high spot of culinary entertaining, Christmas dinner. All of them are designed to employ your microwave as part of your usual system of cooking – with the hob, grill and conventional oven each playing its part. All the dishes and foods mentioned are to be found in the pages of this book.

By cooking in advance and by making use of long standing times and the speedy reheating facility of your microwave oven, you will find yourself planning menus and automatically using the microwave whenever it is convenient.

Spaghetti Bolognese and Stewed Fruit
Prepare the Bolognese sauce in the microwave. While the fruit is cooking in the microwave, boil the spaghetti on the hob. If the fruit is to be accompanied by custard, cook this in the microwave while the spaghetti cooks on the hob, then the fruit can cook in the microwave while the first course is being eaten. Pages 48, 43, 109.

Poached Fish and Vegetables and Fruit Crumble
Prepare the pudding first, microwaving the fruit and then the topping. Either microwave the vegetables and arrange on a covered dish to reheat before serving, or cook some or all of the vegetables on the hob while the pudding and fish are prepared using the microwave oven. The pudding can be reheated whole or in portions just before serving. Pages 74, 109.

Meat Loaf with Jacket Potatoes and Salad and Jam Sponge Pudding
Wash and prick the potatoes. While they cook in the microwave, prepare the meat loaf. Wrap the cooked potatoes tightly in foil. They will keep hot for at least 20 minutes. While the meat loaf cooks in the microwave, assemble the salad. Allow the loaf to stand. Microwave the sponge pudding and allow to stand. Serve the savoury course, reheating the potatoes briefly if necessary. If the pudding

has cooled too much by the time it is served, simply reheat whole or in portions. Pages 44, 56, 124.

A word about cheese and wine

Cheese can be 'ripened' or brought quickly to room temperature in the microwave. Take care not to overheat it though – this is best done on LOW or DEFROST.

Take the chill off red wine: open the bottle, return its cork, heat on HIGH for 15 seconds then decant.

Roast Dinner/Sunday Lunch

It may be a good idea to prepare the starter and the dessert in advance – preferably the day before. Choose a pudding which is served cold, and a starter which can be reheated (such as soup) or which can be assembled quickly before serving (such as melon, grapefruit, pâté or prawn cocktail).

1. In the morning prepare and cook the vegetables separately in the microwave until just tender. Save any juices for the gravy. Arrange them on a serving dish, cover and keep them in a cool place until reheating a few minutes before serving.
2. Weigh the meat and calculate the cooking time on MEDIUM according to how well done you prefer meat. Add to this 20–30 minutes standing time. At the specified time – usually 1–1¾ hours before serving, depending on the weight of the meat – begin cooking the joint following the guidelines on page 79. A microwave thermometer greatly helps you to cook meat to your personal taste. When the correct temperature (page 80) has been reached, remove the joint from the oven and cover securely with foil. Allow to stand for 20 minutes. (The joint will stay hot for 30–40 minutes.)
3. Use the time while the meat is cooking to prepare or assemble starters and/or desserts if liked.
4. Just before serving, reheat the dish of vegetables on HIGH for 3–4 minutes.

5. While the joint is being carved, microwave the gravy, using the vegetable and meat juices.

A useful tip

When family or friends stay for the weekend and plans for an outing are made, I like to be included too. So I cook the joint in advance, sometimes the day before. It is easier to carve cold and can be kept ready, sliced and wrapped in the refrigerator. Then on the day, I microwave the vegetables early, as explained above. I simply make the gravy while the whole meal reheats.

Christmas Dinner

1. *The day before*

   Prepare the stuffing using the microwave to soften the onions (page 71).

   You will probably have cooked the pudding, either by microwave or conventionally, several weeks earlier. However do not despair if you have not. A perfectly acceptable Christmas pudding can be cooked in the microwave the day before. Add a little extra colouring such as treacle or gravy browning, and flavouring such as brandy or rum! (page 108).

   Microwave the bread sauce (page 104) or cranberry sauce (page 104) to save time on the day.

2. *Early on Christmas Day*

   Microwave the potatoes until just cooked. Microwave the vegetables, one type at a time, and arrange them on one or more serving platters. Small quantities of many different vegetables are a real treat and involve the use of only one cooking container. Save the cooking juices for gravy. Cover the vegetables and store them in a cool place.

3. Microwave a sweet sauce to accompany the pudding and cover with wet greaseproof paper.

4. Prepare and stuff the turkey. Weigh it and calculate the cooking time at 6–8 minutes per 450g/1 lb. Add an extra

30 minutes to allow for standing time and keeping hot. Brush the breast with melted, unsalted butter. Wrap foil around the narrow parts of the wings and legs to prevent them drying out – check with your manufacturer's instruction book regarding the use of foil. Place the turkey inside a large roasting bag (or slit one to make it large enough to cover the turkey and tuck underneath), tie loosely and place, breast side down in a large container. Make sure no parts touch the oven wall during cooking. At the calculated time, microwave the turkey for half the cooking time. See the roasting chart on page 80.

5. While the turkey is cooking, you could prepare a cold starter.

6. Turn the bird over, breast side up. Protect the breast bone with a strip of foil. Cook for the remaining time. 15 minutes before the end, drain off all the juices. Finish cooking and wrap the turkey with foil and allow to stand for 30–50 minutes.

7. Meanwhile, roast the microwave-cooked potatoes in a very hot conventional oven. Crisp some bacon rashers and sausages at the same time. If a crisp skin is preferred on the turkey allow the standing time to take place in the hot oven – remove the foil before putting in the oven.

8. Make the gravy in the microwave (page 105).

9. *Finally*
Reheat the vegetables in the microwave and warm the plates in the conventional oven or in a bowl of hot water while the turkey is being carved, (hopefully, by someone else!) and the cold starter is being eaten.

10. Reheat the sweet sauce (on LOW if possible) while the main course is being eaten. Reheat the pudding, either whole or in individual portions, between courses.

Stuffing: Parsley and Lemon

Serves 4–6

	Met.	Imp.
Onion, finely chopped	1 medium	1 medium
Butter	25g	1 oz
Mushrooms, chopped (optional)	50g	2 oz
Breadcrumbs, fresh	100g	4 oz
Egg, beaten	1	1
Parsley, chopped	2 x 15ml sp	2 tbsp
Lemon, grated rind and juice	½	½
Salt and pepper		

Method
1. Put the onion in a suitable container, cover and cook on HIGH for 3 minutes.
2. Stir in the butter until it melts, then mix in the remaining ingredients.
3. Use the stuffing to stuff poultry, meat or fish; or to serve separately, cook on HIGH for 1–2 minutes.

Stuffing: Sage and Onion

Serves 4–6

	Met.	Imp.
Onions, chopped	2 large	2 large
Butter	25g	1 oz
Breadcrumbs, fresh	100g	4 oz
Dried sage	2 x 5ml sp	2 tsp
Egg	1	1
Salt and pepper		

Method
As for Parsley and Lemon.

Serve with poultry or pork.

FISH

Fish stays beautifully whole during microwave cooking. The texture and flavour are rather special too. The fish is cooked very quickly, in the least amount of liquid so that all the flavour is kept in.

HINTS FOR MICROWAVING FISH

Always cover fish during cooking to keep in the juices, except fish coated with breadcrumbs. I would not recommend cooking breadcrumbed or battered fish in the microwave. They will be soggy, not crisp. Fish fingers are successful though. Turn to page 36 for details of how to cook them.

Roasting bags and 'boil-in-the' bags are useful for cooking fish (see page 24). Remember to pierce them to allow steam to escape.

Microwaving is particularly suitable for fish recipes which

call for poaching. The quantity of liquid needed can be reduced. Use only as much as you will need to make a sauce. When no sauce is required no liquid needs to be added.

When cooking whole fish, overlap the tails or the thin ends. This produces an even layer of fish which is more likely to cook evenly. Alternatively wrap the tails in foil to protect them from the microwaves. Check with your instruction book on the use of foil in your particular model.

If the skin is left on whole fish during cooking – pierce it in one or two places to allow steam to escape and to prevent it bursting.

Fish cooked in a sauce is best cooked on MEDIUM or LOW – again to encourage even cooking since the extra liquid attracts the microwaves first.

Add salt *after* cooking. It tends to dry out the surface of the fish during cooking.

Butter or fat can be added if liked to enhance the flavour.

Turn the container once or twice during cooking in ovens without turntables. Stir seafood and quick-cooking ingredients into a dish towards the end of the cooking period e.g. add the fish to a pilaff during the final 5 minutes of cooking.

Though fish can be reheated on LOW it is better to avoid doing so – fish easily over-cooks to become dry and rubbery. Fish is cooked when the flakes separate easily when eased apart with a fork.

When a brown finish is required on fish, use a browning dish pre-heated according to instructions.

Defrosting fish fillets is only necessary if you have to carry out extra preparation such as skinning or adding bread-crumbs or batter. 450g/1 lb fish fillets take about 3–4 minutes on DEFROST, a defrosting-standing time of 5 minutes, 2–3 minutes more and a further standing time of 5 minutes. Where no preparation is needed fillets may be cooked from frozen. The cooking time will of course be longer so check the fish often to avoid over-cooking of thinner areas. To separate fillets microwave on DEFROST for 1–2 minutes.

Whole fish need defrosting before cooking or thinner areas will over-cook while thicker areas remain frozen. See your instruction book for times in your particular oven.

Fish Cooking Time Guide

Cook fish in a covered container on HIGH.

Whole fish: 4–6 minutes per 450g/1 lb

Fillets and steaks: 2–3 minutes for thick fillets
1–2 minutes for thin fillets.

Allow a standing time of 5 minutes.

All the instructrions in these recipes assume the fish has been gutted or prepared.

RECIPES

Fish: Poached

1. Arrange the fish in a suitable container.
2. Add 2–3 x 15ml sp/2–3 tbsp water, fruit juice, wine etc.
3. Dot with butter if liked and season with pepper and add slices of lemon.
4. Cover and cook on HIGH for 1–3 minutes for fillets, depending on their thickness, 2–4 minutes for thick cutlets or rolled fillets, or 4–6 minutes for whole fish or per 450g/1 lb larger fish.
5. Allow a standing time of 5 minutes. Season with salt. Serve with a sauce such as Parsley, recipe on page 103, or Hollandaise opposite.

Hint: Salty fish such as smoked haddock needs extra water or milk to absorb the salt. Pour over sufficient boiling water to cover the fish. The microwave cooking time may be a little longer since the extra water absorbs the microwaves first. (If more than 550ml/1 pt of water is being used, boil it in the kettle. This is more economical and quicker than boiling large amounts of water by microwaving.)

Hollandaise Sauce

Usually a difficult, time-consuming sauce to make, hollandaise is quickly prepared by the microwave method.

	Met.	Imp.
Butter	100g	4 oz
Lemon juice or vinegar	2 x 15ml sp	2 tbsp
Egg yolks	2	2
Salt and pepper		

Method
1. Place the butter into a suitable container and microwave on HIGH for 1 minute or until melted.
2. Add the lemon juice or vinegar, egg yolks and seasoning.
3. Whisk the mixture well.
4. Microwave on HIGH for 30 seconds and whisk well. Continue cooking for 15 seconds at a time and whisking well, until the sauce is thick and creamy. Take care not to over-cook or the sauce will separate.
5. Serve with poached fish, particularly salmon.

Fish: Stuffed

Serves 2

	Met.	Imp.
Whole fish such as trout	2 x 175g	2 x 6 oz
Salt and pepper		
Stuffing, such as Parsley and Lemon (page 71)		
Butter	25g	1 oz

Method
1. Season the fish cavities lightly with salt and pepper and fill them with the stuffing mixture. Slit the skin in two or three places.

2. Arrange the fish on a suitable plate with their tails overlapping.
3. Microwave the butter on HIGH for 1 minute or until melted and brush it over the fish.
4. Cover and cook on HIGH for 4–7 minutes or until the fish flakes when tested with a fork.
5. Allow a standing time of 5 minutes before serving.

Trout with Almonds

Serves 4

	Met.	Imp.
Trout	4 x 175g	4 x 6 oz
Butter, melted	25–50g	1–2 oz
Lemon slices		
Toasted almonds, see page 132		

Method
1. Wash, dry and season the cavities of the fish, adding some butter and lemon slices if liked.
2. Slit the skins in two or three places.
3. Arrange the fish around the outer edge of a large plate, overlapping the tail ends to produce a more even layer of fish.
4. Brush with melted butter, cover and microwave on HIGH for 6–8 minutes. Allow the fish to stand for 5 minutes then sprinkle over some toasted almonds.

Handy hint: Protect heads and tails with strips of foil, particularly if the fish are to be transferred to another plate for serving. Check with your instruction book regarding the use of foil.

MEAT AND POULTRY

Microwave cooking is a very clean method of cooking meat and poultry, with fewer of the messy dishes which are left after conventional cooking. Other advantages include speed of cooking, retention of flavour, and usually less shrinkage. Of course, we all know that joints and whole poultry will not have the brown crisp exterior of their conventionally roasted equivalents. However there are many ways of overcoming this comparatively small problem. Large joints do brown naturally to some degree and the use of roasting bags helps this process. Turn to page 23 et seq. for more information on browning. Brushing with unsalted butter also produces good results.

Use your microwave oven to defrost meat and poultry too. Check with your manufacturer's instruction book for methods and times. Always make sure that meat is *completely* defrosted before cooking. You *must* allow the recommended defrosting-standing time before cooking.

GENERAL HINTS FOR COOKING MEAT

Choose even-shaped pieces of meat to encourage even cooking.

Prevent over-cooking of thinner areas of joints or wing-tips etc. of poultry by covering them with small pieces of foil. Your instruction book will tell you whether you are able to use foil in your particular model.

Arrange smaller pieces of meat like chops with the thicker ends towards the outside of the container.

Mince mixtures can be shaped into balls, burgers or ring moulds to speed up cooking and so that they cook evenly.

Cover meat and poultry during cooking to prevent splashes on the oven wall and to keep moisture in.

Secure meat with wooden (not metal) skewers or string.

Boiling joints such as bacon are suitable for microwave cooking, but instead of immersing the joint in water it is cooked in a roasting bag. (See page 81.)

Braising and Pot Roasting can be done in the microwave. (See page 86.) Microwave ovens with variable controls take gentle, slow cooking in their stride. Beef cuts such as topside, and silverside need tenderising in liquid. In fact less liquid is needed in the microwave since there is less evaporation. Consequently the meat juices are concentrated and very tasty. Braising and pot roasting should be completed on MEDIUM, DEFROST or LOW in a covered container. Check with your instruction book.

Casseroles and Stews generally need less liquid since there is less evaporation. Cut meat into even-sized pieces. If possible use a browning dish to brown the meat before adding the other ingredients. This improves the flavour and the finished appearance of a casserole. Alternatively, brown the meat quickly in a frying pan before adding it to the casserole. The less tender cuts of meat which are used for casseroles are best microwaved on LOW, DEFROST or MEDIUM (after an initial period on HIGH to heat up all the ingredients) to imitate the long, slow cooking of conventional casseroling. Develop the flavour even further by cooking the casserole one day and reheating it the next. During cooking and reheating food flavours have a chance to develop and intermingle.

Frying and grilling. Meats which are suitable for these cooking methods, such as steaks, chops and beefburgers are best microwaved using a browning dish to sear and brown them.

Pies with a meat filling cannot be cooked in the microwave but cooked pies reheat very well (see pages 83 and 136). Prepare pie fillings in the microwave for finishing off in the conventional oven.

Roasting in the microwave is particularly suited to even-shaped joints (particularly those without a bone). They may be cooked in a roasting bag or on a roasting rack and covered with a split roasting bag. The meat should not sit in its own juices. A microwave thermometer (see page 14) is an excellent investment if you plan to cook meat joints in the microwave. You can cook the meat to perfection. Cooking beef so that its centre is still pink is simple and works every time. Overleaf is a useful guide to internal temperatures of cooked meat and their approximate cooking times. The chart includes cooking times on HIGH, but if time is available you may prefer to cook on MEDIUM.

Turn meat joints over, halfway through cooking.

Allow a standing time of 15 minutes or more after cooking to allow the internal temperature to settle down. Cover with foil during this standing time. Use the time to cook vegetables or make gravy in the microwave.

Turn to page 88 for the general method for roasting poultry.

Roasting Chart

Meat		Remove from microwave	Temperature after standing	Approximate cooking time per 450g / 1 lb on HIGH
Beef,	rare	49°C/120°F	60°C/140°F	5–6 minutes
	medium	60°C/140°F	71°C/160°F	6–7 minutes
	well done	71°C/160°F	77°C/170°F	8–9 minutes
Lamb,	medium	66°C/150°F	77°C/170°F	8–9 minutes
	well done	71°C/160°F	82°C/180°F	9–10 minutes
Pork	well done, bacon	82°C/180°F	88°C/190°F	9–10 minutes
Veal		66°C/150°F	77°C/170°F	9 minutes
Chicken		82°C/180°F	88°C/190°F	7 minutes
Turkey		79°C/175°F	90°C/195°F	6–8 minutes

Roly Poly Puddings

Filled with bacon or other meats these savoury puddings cook well in the microwave. They should be wrapped in non-stick or greased greaseproof paper – loosely to allow the pudding to rise. Twist the 'Christmas cracker' ends to close them. Microwave on MEDIUM for about 15 minutes. Allow a standing time of 5 minutes before testing by inserting a skewer. If it comes out clean the pudding is cooked. If not, microwave on MEDIUM for a further 2–3 minutes before allowing it to stand again.

Suet Puddings

Suet puddings cook quickly by microwaves and this eliminates the traditional steamy kitchen associated with cooking suet crust pastry. The pudding lid may harden slightly but cooking the filling (such as steak and kidney or bacon) before adding it to the pastry, produces a softer, more moist result. The filled pudding should be covered and cooked on HIGH for 10 minutes. Allow a standing time of 5 minutes. If the pastry is not quite cooked (test it by easing an area open with a fork), microwave for a minute before standing the pudding again.

RECIPES

Bacon: 'Boiled'

1. Place the bacon joint in a large saucepan and cover with cold water. Bring to the boil slowly on the hob, then discard the water. This removes some of the saltiness.
2. Place the bacon joint in a roasting bag and tie loosely to allow the steam to escape. Sit the joint on a cooking rack or upturned dish.
3. Cook on HIGH or MEDIUM, turning the joint over halfway through cooking. A 1.35kg/3 lb joint of bacon takes 25–30 minutes on HIGH or 30–40 minutes on MEDIUM. If using a microwave thermometer, see opposite for a guide

to the internal temperatures of cooked meat.
4. Wrap the bacon in foil and allow a standing time of 15 minutes.

Beef Olives

The appearance of this dish is improved if a browning dish is used to colour the meat after stage 1. Alternatively, brown the olives in a frying pan before microwave cooking.

Serves 4

	Met.	*Imp.*
Half the quantity of parsley and lemon stuffing, page 71		
Beef topside, thin slices	4	4
Beef stock, boiling	500ml	1 pt
Salt and pepper		
Parsley, chopped	2 x 15ml sp	2 tbsp
Cornflour		

Method
1. Spread the stuffing over the slices of topside and roll them up. Secure with string or thread.
2. Arrange the beef rolls in a suitable, shallow container and pour round sufficient boiling stock to come halfway up their sides.
3. Cover and cook on MEDIUM (for best results) for about one hour or until the meat is just tender. The cooking time will depend on the thickness of the beef.
4. Allow a standing time of 10–15 minutes before removing the meat from the stock.
5. Season the gravy with salt and pepper and stir in the parsley.
6. Thicken the gravy by mixing a little cornflour with a little cold water and stirring this into the stock. Bring to the boil on HIGH.
7. Pour the gravy over the meat to serve.

Beef Pie

Prepare the filling in the microwave – such as Savoury Minced Beef (page 48) or Beef in Red Wine (below) or Beef Stew (overleaf). When converting your own recipes use less liquid than normal and if necessary add extra thickening towards the end of cooking. Mix some flour with a little cold stock/water/wine etc. to make a smooth paste. Add a little of the hot liquid from the meat and stir. Return this mixture to the meat and stir. Microwave on HIGH for a minute or two to cook the flour.

Top the meat with a pastry crust and cook the pie in the conventional oven. Results in the microwave are not acceptable – the filling bubbles over and the pastry does not crisp or brown. Save time by bulk cooking the filling in the microwave and freezing it. Why not batch cook pastry circles or shapes to fit your favourite dish? Freeze them ready for topping a pie filling at a moment's notice. Pies reheat well in the microwave but take care not to overdo it or the pastry becomes soggy.

Beef in Red Wine (or Beef Bourgignon or Burgundy Beef)

Serves 4

	Met.	Imp.
Onions, chopped	175g	6 oz
Garlic clove, crushed	1–2	1–2
Streaky bacon, chopped	100g	4 oz
Cooking oil	1 x 15ml sp	1 tbsp
Braising beef, cut into cubes	700g	1½ lb
Flour, seasoned with salt and pepper	2 x 15ml sp	2 tbsp
Bouquet garni	1	1
Red wine	300ml	½ pt
Button mushrooms	100g	4 oz

Method
1. Place the onions, garlic, bacon and cooking oil into a suitable, large container, cover and cook on HIGH for 3 minutes.
2. Toss the meat in the seasoned flour – this is most easily done in a polythene bag. Stir the meat in the onion mix.
3. Mix in the bouquet garni and red wine.
4. Cover and cook on HIGH for 10 minutes or until the mixture boils, then switch to MEDIUM for about 50 minutes or until the meat is tender, stirring once or twice during cooking.
5. Stir in the mushrooms and cook on HIGH for 2–3 minutes.
6. Allow a standing time of 10 minutes before serving.

Handy hint: If your oven does not have variable power this dish can be made, using the more tender sirloin steak. At step 4, cover and cook on HIGH for 10–15 minutes, and then follow steps 5 and 6.

Beef Stew

Serves 4

	Met.	Imp.
Onion, chopped	1 medium	1 medium
Vegetables such as carrots, leeks, celery, turnip, parsnip, swede	450g	1 lb
Cooking oil	1–2 x 15ml sp	1–2 tbsp
Braising steak, cut into cubes	450g	1 lb
Flour	2 x 15ml sp	2 tbsp
Mixed dried herbs	1 x 15ml sp	1 tbsp
Beef stock, hot	300ml	½ pt
Mustard powder	2 x 5 ml sp	2 tsp
Tomato purée	2 x 15ml sp	2 tbsp

Method

1. Place the onion, vegetables and cooking oil into a suitable, large container. Cover and cook on HIGH for 5 minutes, stirring once.
2. Add the braising steak and cook on HIGH for 5 minutes.
3. Stir in the flour then the remaining ingredients.
4. Cover and microwave on MEDIUM or DEFROST for about 50 minutes or until the beef is tender. Stir two or three times during cooking.
5. Allow a standing time of 10–15 minutes before serving.

Beef Stew with Dumplings

Serves 4

	Met.	Imp.
Ingredients for Beef Stew as opposite		
Dumplings:		
Self-raising flour	225g	8 oz
Salt	1 x 5ml sp	1 tsp
Suet, shredded	100g	4 oz
Mixed dried herbs (optional)	½ x 5ml sp	½ tsp

Method

1. Prepare the beef stew as described in the recipe above.
2. While it is cooking, prepare the dumplings. Sieve together the flour and salt and stir in the suet and herbs if used. Mix with cold water to form a stiff dough. Divide the dough into 8–12 dumplings.
3. Add the dumplings to the cooked stew for the final 10 minutes of cooking.

Bolognese Sauce: Use the recipe for Savoury Minced Beef, page 48.

Braised Beef or Pot Roast

Topside and silverside are the joints which are most suitable.

1. Place the meat and liquid (about 300ml/½ pt) in a suitable covered container or roasting bag, tied loosely and sitting in a suitable container.
2. Cook on MEDIUM for 25–30 minutes per 450g/1 lb, or on DEFROST or LOW for 40–45 minutes per 450g/1 lb. If you have time, the slower cooking is better. Halfway through cooking, turn the joint over and, for a pot roast, add diced or sliced vegetables such as carrot, onion, leek, celery etc. If possible, use a microwave thermometer to tell you when the meat is ready for standing. See the chart on page 80 for the correct temperatures.
3. Allow a standing time of 15 minutes before serving.

Chicken Casserole

Use the recipe for Beef Stew, replacing the beef with 4 chicken portions at stage 2, and the beef stock with chicken stock at stage 3 (page 84).

4. Cover and cook on HIGH for 20–25 minutes or until the chicken is tender. Stir once or twice.
5. Allow a standing time of 10 minutes before serving.

Chicken Chasseur

Serves 4

	Met.	Imp.
Chicken portions	4	4
Butter	25g	1 oz
Spring onions, chopped	4	4
Flour, seasoned with salt and pepper	25g	1 oz
Chicken stock, hot	300ml	½ pt

White wine	150ml	¼ pt
Button mushrooms	100g	4 oz
Parsley, chopped	1 x 15ml sp	1 tbsp

Method
1. Arrange the chicken joints in a suitable, large container. Cover and cook on HIGH for 10 minutes, turning them halfway through cooking.
2. In another container, microwave the butter and onions on HIGH for 1-2 minutes.
3. Stir the seasoned flour into the onions and gradually add the hot stock followed by the remaining ingredients.
4. Pour this over the chicken, cover and cook on HIGH for 15 minutes or until the chicken is tender. Turn the chicken once during cooking.
5. Allow a standing time of 10-15 minutes.

Chicken Curry

Serves 4

	Met.	Imp.
Chicken portions	4	4
Sauce:		
Cooking oil	1 x 15ml sp	1 tbsp
Onions, finely chopped	225g	8 oz
Cornflour	2 x 15ml sp	2 tbsp
Garlic, crushed	1-2 cloves	1-2 cloves
Curry paste	2-3 x 15ml sp	2-3 tbsp
Can tomatoes	397g	14 oz
Chicken stock	300ml	½ pt
Lemon juice	2 x 15ml sp	2 tbsp
Sugar	1 x 5ml sp	1 tsp
Salt and pepper		

Method
1. Arrange the chicken in a suitable, large container. Cover

and cook on HIGH for 10 minutes, turning once during cooking.
2. In another container, microwave the cooking oil and onions on HIGH for 3 minutes.
3. Stir in the cornflour then add the remaining ingredients.
4. Pour the mixture over the chicken, cover and cook on HIGH for 15 minutes or until the chicken is tender. Turn the chicken over halfway through cooking.
5. Allow a standing time of 10–15 minutes before serving with rice (see page 45).

Chicken: Roast

1. Wash and dry the chicken well.
2. Brush with melted butter. If liked add soy sauce/yeast extract/paprika/brown sauce to the butter – this gives a rich colour to an otherwise pale chicken and adds flavour too. Season with pepper (not salt).
3. Place the chicken in a roasting bag, breast side down on a roasting rack or upturned plate sitting in a suitable container. Tie the bag loosely (use a piece of string or cotton – *not* a metal tie or an elastic band) to allow steam to escape.
4. Microwave the chicken, turning it over halfway through. Cook for 6–8 minutes per 450g/1 lb on HIGH or
　　　　10–12 minutes per 450g/1 lb on MEDIUM.
Allow a standing time of 15–20 minutes, covered loosely with foil.

For **stuffed chicken**, add 3 minutes to the total cooking time on HIGH or 5 minutes to the total cooking time on MEDIUM For the stuffing, see page 71.

If using a microwave thermometer, place this in the thick part of the leg – between the leg bone and the breast area. Remove the chicken from the microwave when the thermometer reads 82°C/180°F. This will rise to 88°C/190°F during the standing time.

Handy hints: Orange zest, herbs, garlic or bacon rinds placed in the chicken cavity add delicate flavours to the cooked meat.

Curried Meat

Serves 4–6

1. Prepare a curry sauce as in stages 2 and 3 of Chicken Curry (page 87).
2. Stir in 700g/1½ lb lean braising beef, stewing lamb or pork, cut into cubes.
3. Cover and microwave on HIGH for 5 minutes then switch to MEDIUM for 40–50 minutes or until the meat is tender. Pork will usually tenderise more quickly than lamb, and lamb more quickly than braising beef.
4. Allow a standing time of 10 minutes before serving with rice (page 45).

Gammon with Pineapple

Serves 4

1. Trim the rind off 4 gammon steaks (about 150g/6 oz each) and cut into the fat to prevent the steaks from curling up during cooking.
2. Cook on a plate or rack, covered with absorbent paper, on HIGH for about 10 minutes. Turn the steaks over half-way through cooking.
3. Place a drained pineapple ring on each slice and micro-wave on HIGH for 1 minute before serving.

Handy hint: A browning dish gives a good finish to the gammon steaks. Pre-heat the dish according to the instructions. After searing the gammon steaks on both sides, microwave on HIGH for 6–8 minutes then 1 minute with the pineapple.

Heart

Recipes using heart need careful cooking in the microwave – it will tenderise sufficiently if cooked in liquid on MEDIUM for 45 minutes then LOW for 30 minutes or longer.

Kidneys in Sauce

As with conventional cooking, care is needed not to over-cook the kidneys.

Serves 4

	Met.	Imp.
Butter	50g	2 oz
Lambs' kidneys, skinned, halved and cored	8	8
Flour	1 x 15ml sp	1 tbsp
Stock or red wine, or a mixture of the two	150ml	¼ pt
Salt and pepper		
Parsley, chopped	2 x 15ml sp	2 tbsp

Method

1. Microwave the butter on HIGH until it melts and stir in the kidneys.
2. Cover and cook on HIGH, stirring once or twice, for 6–7 minutes.
3. Stir in the flour then gradually add the stock or wine (or a mixture of both), and seasoning.
4. Cover and cook on HIGH, stirring once or twice, until the sauce thickens (2–4 minutes). Stir in the parsley before serving.

Lamb Casserole

Follow the recipe for Beef Stew on page 84 replacing the beef with lamb and the mixed herbs with rosemary (if liked).

Lamb Crown Roast – with stuffing

Use two pieces of best end of neck or loin. You will need about 12 chops to make a circle and this will serve 6 people. Ask your butcher to chop through the thick ends of the chops so that the pieces will curve.

1. Trim the top 2.5cm/1 in of each bone, cutting off meat and fat. If you like, chop these trimmings finely to mix into the stuffing.
2. Using a trussing needle and string, join the two pieces of lamb, skin side in, to form a crown.
3. Season with pepper. The tips of the bones may be covered with small amounts of foil to prevent the meat ends from over-cooking. Check with your instruction book first though and do not allow foil to touch the sides of the oven.
4. Place the joint on a roasting rack in a shallow container and cover with a slit-open roasting bag.
5. *Either* cook on HIGH for 9–10 minutes per 450g/1 lb *or* microwave on HIGH for 5 minutes then cook on MEDIUM for 15 minutes per 450g/1 lb. Halfway through cooking, baste the joint and fill the centre with stuffing (page 71), pressing down firmly. If using a microwave thermometer, check page 80 for the correct internal temperature.
6. Cover with foil and allow the crown to stand for 15–20 minutes.

Lamb Guard of Honour

Use two equal-size pieces of best end of neck or loin. Allow two chops per person.

1. Follow steps 1 and 3 for Crown Roast.
2. Place the joints in a large shallow container – facing each other with their smaller bone ends upwards and interlocking. Spoon the stuffing into the cavity underneath. (page 71).

3. Cover with a roasting bag which has been slit open and *either* cook on HIGH for 9–10 minutes per 450g/1 lb *or* cook on HIGH for the first 10 minutes then switch to LOW for 13 minutes per 450g/1 lb. If liked, use a meat thermometer (see page 80 for a guide to the internal temperatures).
4. Cover with foil and allow the meat to stand for 15–20 minutes.

Lamb: Moussaka

Serves 4–6

	Met.	Imp.
Aubergines, sliced	2 medium	2 medium
Salt		
The quantity of Tomato Sauce, page 105		
Lamb, raw, minced or chopped finely	350g	12 oz
White sauce, page 103, using 400ml/¾ pt milk		
Cheese, grated	50g	2 oz
Egg, size 1 or 2, beaten	1	1

Method
1. Slice the aubergines and sprinkle the slices with salt. This will help remove any bitter taste. After 15 minutes, rinse and drain the slices.
2. Prepare the tomato sauce, adding the lamb at stage 3.
3. Prepare the white sauce and stir in the cheese. When the sauce is smooth, stir in the beaten egg.
4. Arrange the meat sauce and aubergine slices in layers in a suitable, deep container and top with the cheese sauce.
5. Cover and cook on HIGH for 15 minutes, turning the dish two or three times if your oven does not have a turntable.
6. Brown under a hot grill (make sure the container is suitable) before serving.

Liver and Bacon

Using a browning dish improves the finished colour of liver without a sauce.

Serves 4

	Met.	Imp.
Butter	25g	1 oz
Lambs' liver, cut into thin slices	450g	1 lb
Flour seasoned with salt and pepper	1 x 15ml sp	1 tbsp
Back bacon rashers	4	4

Method
1. Melt the butter on HIGH in a suitable container (30 seconds – 1 minute).
2. Coat the liver with seasoned flour and stir it into the butter.
3. Cover and cook on HIGH for 2–3 minutes.
4. Add the bacon rashers and cook uncovered on HIGH for about 2 minutes.
5. Cover and allow it to stand for 5 minutes. If necessary cook for a further ½–1 minute and stand again.

Liver and Bacon with Sauce

Serves 4

	Met.	Imp.
Butter	25g	1 oz
Onion, chopped	1	1
Lambs' liver, thinly sliced	450g	1 lb
Flour seasoned with salt and pepper	1–2 x 15ml sp	1–2 tbsp
Beef stock, hot	150ml	¼ pt
Dried sage	½ x 5ml sp	½ tsp

Method

1. Microwave the butter and onion on HIGH in a suitable, covered container for 3 minutes.
2. Coat the liver in the seasoned flour then stir it into the onion mixture with the hot stock and sage.
3. Cover and cook on HIGH for about 10 minutes.
4. Allow a standing time of 10 minutes.

Oxtail

Always cook oxtail using the conventional method. It does not tenderise sufficiently in the microwave.

Pork Casserole

Follow the recipe for Beef Stew on page 84, replacing the beef with pork and the mixed herbs with sage (if liked). At stage 4 *either* cook on HIGH for 5 minutes then switch to MEDIUM for 30–40 minutes, stirring once or twice or, *alternatively,* cook on HIGH for 20 minutes. Adding a peeled, cored and sliced cooking apple for the final 10 minutes of cooking time makes the casserole 'special'.

VEGETABLES

Fresh vegetables from the microwave have a lovely colour and flavour and you can cook them to that cooked-yet-crisp stage which is perfect.

HINTS FOR MICROWAVING VEGETABLES
Choose good quality vegetables. Old vegetables dry out and toughen in the microwave.

Personal taste will dictate whether you prefer to cook cauliflower and broccoli by microwaves or conventionally.

Use the minimum amount of water. 30–45ml/2–3 tbsp is usually sufficient for cooking most vegetables.

Cut or trim vegetables into small, uniform pieces to encourage even cooking.

Prick the skins of whole vegetables such as potatoes and

prick tomatoes. This helps prevent them bursting as a result of a steam build-up inside.

Arrange whole vegetables such as potatoes in a circle – one placed in the centre will cook very slowly.

Stir or shake vegetables once or twice during microwaving to encourage even cooking. Turn over large items such as whole potatoes halfway through cooking.

Season vegetables with salt *after* cooking as it tends to draw out their moisture, causing them to dry on the surface.

Always cover vegetables to retain moisture and flavour.

Roasting bags and 'boil-in-the' bags are useful for cooking vegetables. Remember to pierce them or leave the opening loose to allow steam to escape.

Cook vegetables on HIGH and allow a 3–5 minutes' standing time before serving.

Different vegetables can be cooked together so long as they have similar cooking times. Check with the cooking chart in your instruction/recipe book. Alternatively, add quick-cooking vegetables towards the end of the cooking period.

Frozen vegetables need no defrosting before cooking.

Blanching vegetables is possible in your microwave oven. Small quantities (450g/1 lb) at a time are suitable. Check with your instruction book (or 'Out of the Freezer into the Microwave' – another Paperfront) for details.

RECIPES

Cauliflower with Cheese Sauce

Cauliflower cooks best in the microwave when cut into florets.

Serves 4

1. Place 450g/1 lb florets into a suitable container with 3 x 15ml sp/3 tbsp water.
2. Cover and microwave on HIGH for 5–7 minutes, stirring or shaking twice during cooking.
3. Allow a standing time of 5 minutes.
4. Prepare the cheese sauce as described on page 103.
5. Drain the cauliflower, season to taste and coat with the sauce.
6. If necessary reheat on HIGH for 2–3 minutes.

Cauliflower Cheese with Savoury Bread Rolls: recipe on page 49.

Chestnuts

Shelling chestnuts (to accompany sprouts or to be included in a stuffing) is simple with a microwave. Watch them carefully though – they easily dry up if microwaved for too long.

1. Cut a cross in the skins to prevent them exploding.
2. Microwave on HIGH in an uncovered container for 1–2 minutes, stirring them once.
3. Strip the skins off those which are soft. Microwave those which are not for another 30 seconds or until soft enough to peel.

Herbs: Drying

Dry fresh garden herbs for use with vegetables, meats and poultry, fish, sauces and stuffings.

1. Place washed and dried leaves of fresh herbs on absorbent paper in the microwave alongside a small dish of water. As the moisture is removed from the herbs the bowl of water absorbs the microwaves. Otherwise the

herbs will burn and your oven could be damaged.
2. Microwave uncovered on HIGH for 30 seconds and check them.
3. If they do not feel dry, microwave them for a further 15–30 seconds before checking again.
4. Continue microwaving for 15–30 seconds at a time until the herbs are dry.
5. Allow the herbs to stand for 10 minutes before packing (whole, or crushed) into screw-top jars.

Marrow: Stuffed Rings of

Serves 4

	Met.	Imp.
Savoury Minced Beef, recipe page 48		
Marrow rings, de-seeded	4 x 2½cm	4 x 1 in thick
Water	2 x 5ml sp	2 tsp
Salt and pepper		
Cheese, grated	25–50g	1–2 oz

Method
1. Prepare the Savoury Minced Beef.
2. Arrange the marrow rings in a circle on a large plate. Put ½ x 5 ml sp/½ tsp water in the middle of each.
3. Cover and microwave on HIGH for 6–8 minutes or until they are just tender.
4. Allow to stand for 5 minutes before draining off the water.
5. Season to taste with salt and pepper.
6. Meanwhile microwave the Savoury Minced Beef on HIGH until heated through (5–8 minutes).
7. Pile the mixture into the marrow rings and sprinkle over the grated cheese.
8. Reheat on HIGH for 1–2 minutes if necessary.

Variation: Replace the cheese with tomato sauce, recipe on page 105.

Marrow rings are also good filled with a thick white sauce (page 103) into which has been mixed prawns, tuna, cooked chopped ham or chicken, or mushrooms for example.

Pease Pudding

Serves 4–6

	Met.	Imp.
Split yellow peas	225g	8 oz
Onion, chopped	1 small	1 small
Bacon stock, hot	550–700ml	1–1¼ pt
Black pepper		
Butter	25g	1 oz

Method
1. Pour plenty of boiling water over the split peas, cover them and allow them to stand for 1 hour before using.
2. Drain them and put the peas into a large, deep container with the onion, hot bacon stock and black pepper.
3. Cover and cook on HIGH for 20 minutes or more until the peas are cooked, stirring two or three times during cooking.
4. Remove the cover and boil rapidly on HIGH until the mixture thickens. Continue, stirring frequently, until the peas form the desired consistency.
5. Stir in the butter before serving.

Peppers – Stuffed

Peppers may be stuffed with your favourite filling if they are blanched in boiling water for 2 minutes first (tops and seeds removed).

Serves 2

	Met.	Imp.
Butter	25g	1 oz
Onion, chopped finely	1 large	1 large
Celery, chopped finely	1 stick	1 stick
Mushrooms, chopped	50g	2 oz
Tomato purée	1 x 15ml sp	1 tbsp
French mustard	2 x 5ml sp	2 tsp
Rice, cooked	75g	3 oz
Ham, chicken or other cooked meat, minced or finely chopped	225g	8 oz
Parsley, chopped	1 x 15ml sp	1 tbsp
Salt and pepper		
Peppers, de-seeded and blanched, lids removed	2	2

Method

1. Microwave the butter, onion and celery on HIGH in a suitable, covered container for 3 minutes.
2. Stir in the remaining stuffing ingredients and mix well.
3. Pile the mixture into the peppers and place these in a suitable, buttered container and top them with their lids.
4. Cover and cook on HIGH for 10–12 minutes, turning the dish at least once if your oven does not have a turntable.
5. Allow the peppers to stand for 5 minutes before serving.

Serving suggestion: Serve with tomato sauce, page 105.

Variation: This recipe can also be made using the Savoury Minced Beef on page 48 to stuff the peppers.

Potato Chips
Deep frying must never be attempted in the microwave. However, chips are crisper if par-cooked in the microwave before deep-frying on the hob. See page 41.

Potatoes: in their Jackets: See page 44

Potatoes: Roast

Potatoes cannot be roasted in the microwave – they will not crisp and brown sufficiently even with a browning dish. However you can save time and fuel by par-cooking them in the microwave (on HIGH for about 5 minutes) before adding them to the roasting tin. This method produces really crisp potatoes.

SAUCES AND GRAVY

Sauces and gravy add flavour, moisture and a contrast in texture to many dishes. Made in the microwave they do not stick or burn on their containers as sauces are liable to do in a saucepan on the hob. For this reason small quantities are made easily.

HINTS FOR SAUCE-MAKING
Make sauces in a serving jug for convenience. Large quantities can be made in a bowl or other suitable container. Make sure the container is large enough to hold the sauce without it boiling over. Use a container which allows easy stirring since sauces containing flour or eggs need stirring regularly during cooking to avoid making lumps. (Every $1\frac{1}{2}$–2 minutes is a good guide.)

Dissolve cornflour with a little cold liquid before stirring into hot ingredients.

Sauces and gravy which normally require fast boiling to reduce them should have extra thickening added, since there is less evaporation in the microwave oven.

As with conventional cooking, save the juices from meat, fish and vegetables to make, or stir into, sauces and gravy.

Once a flour- or cornflour-based sauce has thickened, you may like to cook it for a few minutes extra on MEDIUM to help develop its flavour.

Sauces reheat well in the microwave so they may be made in advance. Stir regularly as you microwave on HIGH. If the sauce has thickened during its cooking period add a little extra liquid during reheating.

Defrosting sauces is simple. Cover the container and microwave on DEFROST, breaking up the sauce block with a fork to speed up the process. 550ml/1 pt sauce takes 10–12 minutes. Allow a 5–10 minute defrosting-standing time.

RECIPES

Basic White Sauce *makes just over 1 pt*

	Met.	Imp.
Butter	40g	1½ oz
Flour	40g	1½ oz
Milk	550ml	1 pt
Salt and pepper		

Method
1. Place the butter in a suitable container or jug. Microwave on HIGH for ½–1 minute or until melted.
2. Stir in the flour and gradually add the milk. Season to taste.
3. Microwave, uncovered, on HIGH for 5–6 minutes, stirring two or three times during cooking. Allow a standing time of 5 minutes.

Handy hint: Heating the milk for 3 minutes on HIGH before adding it to the flour and butter mixture produces a very creamy sauce. Having added the hot milk, microwave on HIGH for 2–3 minutes, stirring twice
Parsley Sauce: Add 2–3 x 15ml sp/2–3 tbsp chopped parsley before standing.
Cheese Sauce: Add 75–100g/3–4 oz grated cheese before standing.
Mushroom Sauce: At stage 1 microwave some chopped mushrooms with the butter, covered on HIGH for 2 minutes.
Onion Sauce: At stage 1 microwave some chopped onion in the butter, covered on HIGH for 3 minutes.
Other Variations: Add prawns, chopped anchovies or chopped hard-boiled eggs.

Apple Sauce

Microwave sliced cooking apples on HIGH with 1 tbsp water and 2 tsp sugar, stirring often, until cooked and puréed (about 5 minutes for 225g/8 oz apples). Beat in a knob of butter. Serve with roast pork.

Bread Sauce

	Met.	Imp.
Onion, cut in quarters	1 small	1 small
Bay leaf	1	1
Black peppercorns	6	6
Whole cloves	2	2
Milk	300ml	½ pt
Breadcrumbs	50–75g	2–3 oz
Butter	25g	1 oz
Salt		

Method
1. Place the onion, bay leaf, peppercorns, cloves and milk into a suitable, deep container.
2. Microwave on HIGH for 3 minutes. Cover it and allow a standing time of 5 minutes to allow the flavours to intermingle.
3. Strain the mixture and return the milk to the container.
4. Stir in the breadcrumbs and butter, cover and microwave on HIGH for 2 minutes, stirring once.
5. Season to taste with salt and stir well.
6. Allow the sauce to stand for 10 minutes before serving with chicken or turkey.

Cranberry Sauce

Place 225g/8 oz cranberries in 300ml/½ pt water and bring to the boil on HIGH. Continue cooking on HIGH for about 5 minutes or until the cranberries burst. Sweeten with sugar to taste. Allow the sauce to cool before serving.

Tomato Sauce

Serve this sauce with fish, vegetables, meat or pasta.

	Met.	Imp.
Butter	**15–25g**	½–1 oz
Onion, chopped finely	**1**	1
Can tomatoes, roughly chopped	**397g**	14 oz
Herbs such as basil or oregano	**to taste**	to taste
Salt and black pepper		

Method
1. Microwave the butter on HIGH for 1 minute or until melted.
2. Add the onion, cover and microwave on HIGH for 3 minutes.
3. Stir in the roughly chopped tomatoes (including the juice), herbs and seasoning.
4. Cover and cook on HIGH for 5–8 minutes, stirring at least once.

Handy hint: If a thicker sauce is preferred, stir in a little cornflour at the end of stage 2. If a smoother sauce is preferred, sieve or blend the finished sauce.

Gravy

Make delicious gravy using the juices left after cooking a meat joint. Skim off the fat, leaving the juice with just 1–2 x 15ml sp/1–2 tbsp fat. Stir in 2 x 15ml sp/2 tbsp flour or cornflour and gradually add 550ml/1 pt stock or cooking liquid from the vegetables. Microwave on HIGH for 5–7 minutes, stirring two or three times during cooking. Season to taste with salt and pepper.

Handy hints: If a darker gravy is preferred stir in a little gravy browning. For a thicker or a thinner gravy, adjust the amount of flour.

9

DESSERTS AND PUDDINGS

Delicious puddings and light desserts provide the finishing touches to a meal. Made in the microwave oven they are prepared in very little time and can be even more successful than when cooked conventionally.

HINTS FOR DESSERTS AND PUDDINGS

Custards
Custards for pouring, for trifles or for creamy cold desserts mixed with fruit, chocolate, etc., are simple to make in the microwave oven. If your model has a variable power control, check with the instructions for the best setting on which to cook those custards which contain eggs. In microwave cooking as well as in conventional cooking care must be taken not to overheat and therefore curdle the mixture. See

page 117 for Custard Tart and page 118 for Baked Egg Custard.

Custard and blancmange powders made up in a jug are microwaved in minutes – with no sticky saucepans to wash. Mix the powder with a little of the milk (according to the packet instructions) to form a smooth paste. Gradually stir in the rest of the milk. Microwave on HIGH (7 minutes for 550ml/1 pt) until the custard thickens, stirring two or three times during cooking. Add sugar to taste.

Cheesecakes

Cooked cheesecakes have a good flavour. When converting your own recipe, cook on HIGH and stop cooking when the centre still appears slightly undercooked. The centre will finish cooking during a 10 minute standing time.

Cold cheesecakes are simple. The gelatine or chocolate used as the setting agent is prepared as follows:

Gelatine: Microwave some of the liquid from the ingredients on HIGH until it is hot (but not boiling). Briskly stir in the gelatine powder. Do not allow the mixture to boil or the gelatine will lose its setting quality. Return this to the main mixture.

Chocolate: There is no need for a double boiler or a bowl over a saucepan of hot water. Simply melt chocolate in a bowl in the microwave. Take care not to overheat it – heating on MEDIUM is advisable.

For topping a cheesecake: toast coconut by spreading some desiccated coconut over a large plate and microwave uncovered on HIGH until golden brown. Watch it carefully and stir or shake the coconut every minute to prevent patchy browning and burning. Or, toast some nuts (see page 132).

For biscuit bases see page 114.

Christmas Pudding

Your favourite Christmas pudding recipes will cook in a very short time – saving a good deal of fuel. Do not expect the flavour to be quite as developed as that cooked conventionally. The pudding will not be as dark. Add extra colour in the form of gravy browning or cocoa powder. Use brown sugar in the recipe too. Cover the pudding. A 900ml/1½ pt pudding will take about 10–12 minutes on HIGH. Allow the pudding to rest for 5 minutes halfway through cooking. It can be left to mature for several months wrapped in greaseproof paper and foil. Reheat individual portions in their serving dish for convenience. One portion takes ½–1 minute on HIGH.

Crumble Toppings

These are suitable for microwave cooking though they will not brown or crisp. Sprinkle crumble over cooked fruit which has been sweetened to taste. Cook on HIGH for 5–7 minutes. Allow a standing time of 5 minutes. For a more inviting brown finish, place under a hot grill (if the container is suitable) for a few minutes. Demerara sugar gives a good finish too.

Fruit

Microwaved fruits are juicy and keep their shape beautifully. Their colour and flavour are excellent too since cooking is completed in 1–2 tbsp water and in the shortest possible time. Cook (or cut fruit into) uniform pieces to encourage even cooking. Cover during cooking to retain maximum moisture and flavour. Use less water than in conventional cooking since there is less evaporation.

Place the prepared fruit, with or without sugar and flavourings, into a suitable container. Cover and cook on HIGH, stirring once during cooking if possible. Cooking times will depend on the type of fruit, its quality, its age, its starting temperature and its preparation (whole or sliced).

As a guide: 450g/1 lb soft fruits take 2–5 minutes
450g/1 lb hard fruits take 7–10 minutes

The skins of whole fruits, such as apples, should be split in order to prevent them bursting open during cooking.

Dried fruits re-hydrate and plump up beautifully in a very short time. Dried prunes, apricots, peaches etc. for a fruit salad should be placed in a suitable container. Pour over sufficient water, fruit juice or tea, cover and microwave on HIGH for about 8 minutes. Allow a standing time of 10 minutes before using.

To plump up raisins etc., for puddings and cakes, place them in a suitable container with a little water, orange juice, tea, sherry or wine. Microwave, uncovered, on HIGH for about 3 minutes. Cover and stand for 5 minutes. Cool the fruit before using it.

Citrus fruit rinds can be dried in the microwave and used for flavouring custards, sponges and other desserts, cakes, sauces and stuffings. Spread some grated rind over a large plate. Microwave uncovered on HIGH for about 1 minute. Stir the rind and if it is not dry to the touch, microwave again for 30 seconds. Continue this process carefully then allow the rind to cool before packing it in a screw-top jar.

Meringue Toppings (see also pages 113 and 134)
Meringue toppings on fruit, for example, set well in the microwave but they will not brown and crisp. You may like to brown the microwave-cooked meringue under a hot grill. Alternatively, a sprinkling of toasted coconut (page 108), demerara sugar or toasted nuts (page 132) looks attractive.

Milk Puddings (see also pages 122 and 123)
Your microwave can help you prepare creamy milk puddings such as semolina or ground rice. Rice pudding with whole rice grains should be prepared in a very large container – the milk will rise up its sides dramatically.

Pancakes
These cannot be cooked by microwaves but they reheat most successfully. Prepare fillings such as fruit and nuts in the microwave and use these to fill pancakes which have been cooked in the frying pan. Fill them in advance (keep some in

the freezer too) and simply reheat (or defrost, remembering to include a defrosting-standing time and reheat) just before serving.

Pastry Dishes (see also page 135)
Shortcrust pastry cooks well in the microwave and its flavour is excellent, but it will not brown. When making flans, you may prefer to cook the flan case conventionally and the filling by microwave. Double crust pies are not successful – the bottom layer does not cook and the fruit filling boils out of the top. They reheat well though – but take care – the filling becomes very hot while the pastry remains only warm to the touch.

Suet crust pastry can be cooked by microwaves but it needs to be covered to keep it moist. Take care not to over-cook or the pastry will dry out and toughen.

Puff and flaky pastry do not cook well in the microwave. They need the dry heat of a conventional oven to produce good results. They reheat successfully though.

Soufflés
Hot soufflés do not microwave successfully. They need the external heat of a conventional oven to crisp their surfaces and hold their shape. Ingredients for cold soufflés can be prepared in the microwave e.g. gelatine (page 108), orange and lemon juice (page 31), blanched and toasted nuts (page 132).

Sponge and Suet Puddings (see also pages 124 and 125)
These cook in a few minutes instead of hours of steaming on the hob. The results are impressive too. Cooking is usually completed on HIGH. A sponge pudding takes about 3–6 minutes, and a suet pudding about 5–6 minutes. The pudding should be removed from the oven when it is still slightly moist on top. It will continue cooking during a 5 minute standing time (over-cooking will produce a dry-textured pudding).

Grease pudding basins in the usual way, for easy removal of the cooked pudding. Allow plenty of room for the pudding to rise during microwave cooking – the size increase is instantly dramatic, though the pudding reduces in size when the microwave power is switched off.

When experimenting with your favourite recipes you may need to increase the quantity of liquid since it evaporates quickly. Cover puddings loosely with non-stick or greased greaseproof paper to keep moisture in and to allow the puddings to rise. Turn the cooking pudding once or twice during the microwaving – do not worry, it will rise again and continue cooking when the microwaves are switched back on.

Soften butter in the microwave before mixing sponge puddings or toppings. 100g/4 oz takes about 10 seconds on HIGH.

Soften jams, syrup and honey to top your sponge mixtures. In plastic jars, golden syrup can be softened for easy measuring by heating on HIGH for 20–30 seconds. If a recipe requires clear honey and you have the crystallised sort, microwave it on HIGH to soften and clarify it before using.

RECIPES FOR DESSERTS AND PUDDINGS

Apples: Baked

Microwave-baked apples have a lovely flavour though do not expect their skins to cook like those done traditionally.
1. Core medium-size cooking apples and slit the skin round the middle of each. Arrange in a circle on a plate.
2. Fill their centres with sugar and butter or a mixture of dried fruit, sugar and spices.
3. Microwave, uncovered, on HIGH for 6 8 minutes for four

apples. They should be just cooked but still holding their shape.

4. Allow a standing time of 5 minutes before checking whether they are cooked. If necessary, microwave for an extra 1-2 minutes before standing them again for 5 minutes.

Apple Meringue

Serves 4

	Met.	Imp.
Cooking apples, peeled, cored and sliced	700g	1½ lb
Sugar, granulated	50g	2 oz
Flavouring such as cloves, cinnamon, mixed spice, vanilla, grated orange or lemon rind		
Egg whites	2	2
Caster sugar	100g	4 oz
Flaked almonds, plain or toasted		

Method

1. Place the apple slices in a suitable container with the granulated sugar and flavouring(s). Cook on HIGH for about 5 minutes.
2. Whisk the egg whites until they form stiff peaks then whisk in half the caster sugar.
3. Fold in the remaining caster sugar then spread it over the top of the apples.
4. Sprinkle with flaked (or toasted) almonds and cook, uncovered, on HIGH for about 2 minutes or until the meringue sets firm.
5. Allow a standing time of 5 minutes before serving.

Apple (or Fruit) Pie

Prepare the apple (or fruit) filling in the microwave then cook the pie in the conventional oven. 700g/1½ lb apples which have been peeled, cored and sliced, take about 5 minutes in a covered container on HIGH.

Biscuit Crumb Base or Case

Use this as a base for a cheesecake or a flan case for chilled cream dishes, or jellies.

	Met.	Imp.
Butter	75g	3 oz
Biscuit crumbs (digestive or gingernut)	225g	8 oz
Sugar (optional)	50g	2 oz

Method
1. Microwave the butter in a suitable container on HIGH for 1–2 minutes or until melted.
2. Stir in the biscuit crumbs and sugar if used.
3. Line a suitable 18cm/7 in flan dish with non-stick paper to ensure easy removal of the base or case.
4. To make a base only, press half the mixture over the dish. (Use the other half to make another base for the freezer.) To make a case, press the mixture into the dish to cover the base and sides.
5. Cool in the refrigerator before filling.

Bread and Butter Pudding

Cooking times will vary with different models but, once mastered, the result is excellent.

Serves 4

	Met.	*Imp.*
Bread slices, lightly buttered	6	6
Dried fruit, e.g. sultanas	2–3 x 15ml sp	2–3 tbsp
Milk	400ml	¾ pt
Eggs, size 3	3	3
Caster sugar	40g	1½ oz
Vanilla essence		

Method

1. Arrange the bread slices (cut them if necessary) in a straight-sided soufflé dish, sprinkle each layer with dried fruit.
2. Heat the milk on HIGH for 2–3 minutes until it is hot but not boiling.
3. Beat together the eggs and sugar and stir them into the hot milk. Add a little vanilla essence if liked.
4. Pour this custard over the bread.
5. Place the dish in a larger container with sufficient hot water (from the kettle) to come halfway up the sides of the pudding dish.
6. Follow the cooking method for Baked Egg Custard on page 118.

Bread Pudding

The appearance of this traditional spicy pudding is not so appetising when cooked in the microwave, though the flavour and texture are lovely. A topping of fruit such as sliced apples, brushed with golden syrup, added during the final half of cooking, improves both appearance and flavour. Alternatively brush the top with a jam glaze (page 120) when the pudding has cooled.

Serves 4

	Met.	Imp.
Bread, cut into small pieces	225g	8 oz
Milk	300ml	½ pt
Egg, beaten, size 2	1	1
Butter	50g	2 oz
Mixed spice	2 x 5ml sp	2 tsp
Mixed peel	50g	2 oz
Dried mixed fruit	175g	6 oz
Demerara sugar		

Method
1. Soak the bread pieces in the milk before mixing in the beaten egg, butter (melted in the microwave) and the remaining ingredients (except the demerara sugar).
2. Pour the mixture into a lightly buttered, straight-sided soufflé dish and microwave uncovered on MEDIUM for 10 minutes.
3. Allow the pudding to stand for 10 minutes.
4. Turn the dish if your oven does not have a turntable and microwave again on MEDIUM for a further 10 minutes.
5. Sprinkle the top with demerara sugar and allow it to stand again.

Castle Puddings

Serves 6
1. Butter a six-mould muffin/bun tray and place a spoonful of jam in each.
2. Top with a Victoria Sandwich mixture (see page 134) flavoured with vanilla or almond essence.
3. Microwave covered loosely with non-stick or greased greaseproof paper (the puddings must have room to rise) on HIGH for 2-3 minutes.

4. Allow a standing time of 5 minutes before turning out
   from the tray and serving with custard or cream.

Handy hint: Individual puddings can also be cooked in
suitable buttered cups – one at a time. One pudding will take
about 1 minute.

Chocolate Pudding

Conventional recipes which include the method where
chocolate, butter, sugar and liquid are heated together are
suitable for microwave cooking. Microwave on HIGH for 4–6
minutes. Alternatively use the recipe for Jam Sponge
Pudding on page 124 which combines with the recipe for
Victoria Sandwich on page 134, replacing 1 x 15ml sp/1 tbsp
of the flour with the same quantity of cocoa or chocolate
powder.

Condé: Fruit

Serves 4–6
1. Prepare a rice pudding using the recipe on page 122. Use
   50g/2 oz short grain rice to 550ml/1 pt milk and sugar
   to taste.
2. Allow the pudding to cool before stirring in some double
   cream and chopped fresh or tinned fruit.
3. Chill before serving.

Custard Tart

Serves 4

	Met.	Imp.
Shortcrust pastry case	18cm	7 in
Eggs, size 2	2	2
Caster sugar	40g	1½ oz
Milk	400ml	¾ pt
Nutmeg, grated		

Method
1. *Either* cook the pastry case in the microwave following the directions on page 137.
   Or bake the pastry in the conventional oven.
2. Beat together the eggs and sugar. Stir in the milk.
3. Pour the custard into the pastry case (which should be in a microwave-safe container). Grate some nutmeg over the top.
4. *Either* microwave uncovered on HIGH for 2 minutes then allow to stand for 2 minutes. Microwave again for 1 minute, followed by a 2 minute standing time. Repeat this process until the custard is set.
   Or cook on LOW for 5 minutes, stand for 2 minutes. Microwave again on LOW for 2 minutes, followed by a 2 minute standing time. Repeat this process until the custard is set.

Handy hint: Microwave the custard until it begins to set before pouring it into the pastry case. Finish cooking as above – the time will be shorter so microwave for short periods followed by a standing time.

Egg Custard, Baked

The microwave produces superb baked egg custard once you have mastered the technique and timing to suit your particular model. Check with your instruction book to see which setting it recommends for this dish. See methods below.

Serves 4

	Met.	*Imp.*
Milk	550ml	1 pt
Vanilla essence		
Eggs, size 2	4	4
Caster sugar	40g	1½ oz
Nutmeg, grated		

Method
1. Place the milk in a suitable jug with a few drops of vanilla essence. Microwave on HIGH for 2–3 minutes until hot but not boiling.
2. Beat together the eggs and sugar. Whisk in the hot milk then strain the mixture into a 900ml/1½ pt soufflé dish. Sprinkle over some grated nutmeg.
3. Place the soufflé dish in a large container and pour round sufficient hot water (from the kettle) to come halfway up the sides of the dish.
4. *Either* microwave, uncovered on LOW for about 15 minutes or until lightly set. (Turn the dish every few minutes if your microwave does not have a turntable.) Allow the custard to stand for 5 minutes, before cooking for an extra few minutes if necessary.

   Or microwave, uncovered, on HIGH for 4–5 minutes until the custard is very hot. (Turn the dish once or twice in those microwave ovens without turntables.) Allow it to stand for 5 minutes before checking if the custard is set. If not, cook on HIGH for 1–2 minutes more, allow to stand, then check again. Continue this process until the custard is set.

Fruit Flan

Prepare a shortcrust pastry case. Microwave cooking instructions appear on page 137, or it may be cooked conventionally for a crisp finish.

Fill the case with fresh fruit, fruit cooked in the microwave (see page 109), or drained tinned fruit. Coat with a glaze such as from the next recipe or thicken some fruit juice using gelatine (page 108). Alternatively use arrowroot: mix 1–2 x 5ml sp/ 1–2 tsp arrowroot with a little cold fruit juice in a small container. Microwave, uncovered on HIGH, stirring frequently until the mixture thickens. Pour or brush this over the fruit.

Jam Glaze

Use this for topping fruit, sponge puddings or fruit flans, and for glazing cakes to make an attractive finish. Make sure the container is suitable for high temperature cooking.
1. Place about 100g/4 oz jam, such as apricot, in a bowl with 2 x 5ml sp/2 tsp lemon juice and 1 x 15ml sp/1 tbsp water.
2. Bring to the boil by microwaving, uncovered, on HIGH.
3. Sieve the mixture and allow to cool.

Lemon Curd

Makes about 900g/2 lb

	Met.	Imp.
Lemons, grated rind and juice	4	4
Butter, unsalted	100g	4 oz
Caster sugar	450g	1 lb
Eggs, size 2, beaten	4	4

Method
1. Mix together the lemon rind and juice, butter and sugar in a suitable container and microwave on HIGH for 4 minutes.
2. Stir the mixture well to dissolve the sugar and to mix in the melted butter.
3. Add the beaten eggs and stir well.
4. Microwave, uncovered, on HIGH for 5–6 minutes, stirring every minute until the mixture is thick and creamy.
5. Cool slightly before potting.

Lemon Meringue Pie

Best results are obtained if the pastry is cooked conventionally, though microwaving pastry (see page 137) is acceptable. Cook the lemon base in the microwave first, about 3 minutes on HIGH, allowing it to cool slightly before adding egg yolks. Pour this into the pastry case and top with meringue (see page 134). Cook on MEDIUM for 3–4 minutes then brown under the grill.

Macaroni Pudding

Serves 4

	Met.	*Imp.*
Macaroni	175g	6 oz
Milk	550ml	1 pt
Sugar	40g	1½ oz

Method
1. Place the macaroni, milk and sugar in a large, deep microwave container. It will rise considerably during cooking.
2. Cover and cook on HIGH for 10–15 minutes, stirring twice during cooking.
3. Allow the pudding to stand, covered, for 10 minutes. Stir well before serving.

Queen of Puddings

This will not have its usual characteristic brown top but is easily 'disguised' by sprinkling it with chopped, toasted nuts. Alternatively, brown it under a hot grill after microwave cooking.

Serves 4

	Met.	Imp.
Milk	400ml	¾ pt
Butter	25g	1 oz
Eggs, size 3, separated	2	2
Caster sugar	50g	2 oz
Lemon, rind of	½	½
Breadcrumbs	75g	3 oz
Jam	2 x 15ml sp	2 tbsp

Method

1. Mix together the milk, butter, egg yolks, half the sugar and lemon rind in a suitable jug.
2. Microwave on HIGH for 2½–3 minutes, stirring once or twice.
3. Pour this over the breadcrumbs in a suitable dish.
4. Melt the jam in the microwave on HIGH for 30 seconds and trickle it over the breadcrumb mix.
5. Whisk the egg whites until they form stiff peaks, then whisk in half the remaining sugar. Fold in the rest of the sugar then pile the meringue on top of the jam.
6. Microwave, uncovered, on HIGH for 4–5 minutes or until the meringue is set.

Rice Pudding

Rice pudding cooked by microwaves is deliciously creamy.

Serves 4

	Met.	Imp.
Milk	550ml	1 pt
Short grain rice/ pudding rice	50g	2 oz
Sugar	40g	1½ oz
Butter		
Nutmeg, grated		

Method
1. Place the milk, rice and sugar in a suitable, deep container (the pudding must have a lot of space to boil up).
2. Dot the pudding with butter and sprinkle with grated nutmeg.
3. Bring to the boil by cooking on HIGH for about 5 minutes. Stir well.
4. Cover and cook on LOW for 30–35 minutes or until cooked and beginning to thicken, stirring every 10 minutes.
5. Allow a standing time of 5 minutes before serving.

Handy hint: If you prefer a pudding with a skin on top, transfer it to a suitable container and brown the top gently under the grill.

Semolina Pudding

Serves 4

	Met.	*Imp.*
Milk	550ml	1 pt
Semolina	4 x 15ml sp	4 tbsp
Caster sugar		

Method
1. Place the milk, semolina and sugar to taste into a suitable, deep container. The mixture must have plenty of room to rise.
2. Microwave on HIGH for about 5 minutes or until boiling.
3. Stir well, microwave until boiling again, then cover and cook on LOW for about 10 minutes, stirring once or twice.
4. Allow the pudding to stand for 5 minutes before serving.

Sponge Pudding: Jam

Serves 4

1. Place 2-3 x 15ml sp/2-3 tbsp jam into a buttered 1.1 litre/ 2 pt basin. Top with a quantity of Victoria Sandwich mix (page 134).
2. Cover loosely with non-stick or greased greaseproof paper (the pudding must have space to rise) and microwave on HIGH for 5-6 minutes. It should look slightly moist on the surface.
3. Stand the pudding for 5 minutes before turning out from the basin.

Spotted Dick

This pudding is cooked in a roasting bag or microwave cooking bag.

Serves 4

	Met.	*Imp.*
Mixed dried fruit	50g	2 oz
Suet, shredded	50g	2 oz
Sugar	25g	1 oz
Salt	pinch	pinch
Self-raising flour, sifted	100g	4 oz
Milk		

Method

1. Mix the dried fruit, suet, sugar, salt and flour.
2. Stir in sufficient milk to make a slack dough.
3. Place the mixture in a roasting bag or microwave bag. Tie the opening loosely (use a piece of string or a strip of the bag, cut off from the end) to allow the pudding to expand and steam to escape.
4. Place the bag in a large container with 550ml/1 pt boiling water (from the kettle) – tied end upwards, out of the water.

5. Cover and microwave on HIGH for 12–15 minutes, turning the pudding if possible halfway through cooking.
6. Allow the pudding to stand for 5 minutes before draining and serving with custard.

Strawberry Shortcake

Shortbread cooks splendidly in the microwave and is very suitable for decoration with fruit and cream since its surface will be quite pale. The recipe appears on page 139. When the shortbread is cool, decorate it with whipped cream and fresh strawberries. Use other fresh fruits in season too – such as raspberries, blackberries or peaches.

Suet Pudding with Jam

Serves 4

	Met.	*Imp.*
Jam	2–3 x 15ml sp	2 tbsp
Self-raising flour	100g	4 oz
Salt	pinch	pinch
Caster sugar	50g	2 oz
Suet, shredded	50g	2 oz
Egg, beaten	1	1
Milk		

Method
1. Put the jam into the base of a buttered 900ml/1½ pt pudding basin.
2. Sieve together the flour and salt. Stir in the sugar, suet, egg and sufficient milk to form a soft mixture.
3. Top the jam with the suet mixture and cover loosely.
4. Microwave on LOW for 6–9 minutes or until the surface of the pudding springs back into shape when pressed gently with your fingers.

5. Allow a standing time of 5 minutes before turning out of the basin.

Ring the changes: Replace the jam with marmalade, honey, syrup, stewed fruit such as apples or rhubarb, canned fruit or pie fillings.

Summer Pudding

Prepare the fruits for this in the microwave. Follow the hints on page 109.

Serves 4-6
1. Line a buttered 900ml/1½ pt pudding basin with bread slices (trimmed of their crusts).
2. Microwave soft fruits such as raspberries and redcurrants with sugar to taste. (See page 109 for times.)
3. Drain off some of the cooking liquid and reserve this for serving with the pudding.
4. Fill the pudding with fruit and cover with more bread, right to the edges.
5. Put a plate on top of the pudding and a weight on top of that. Chill overnight before turning out or serving from the basin with the reserved juice.

Treacle Tart

This works best when the flan case is made with a rich shortcrust pastry and this must be cooked in the conventional oven. Keep a supply in the freezer.

Serves 4-6

	Met.	*Imp.*
Golden syrup	6 x 15ml sp	6 tbsp
Breadcrumbs	50g	2 oz
Lemon juice and grated		
lemon rind	little	little
Flan case, cooked	20cm	8 in

Method

1. Mix together the golden syrup and the breadcrumbs and stir in a little lemon juice and rind.
2. Spread the mixture over the base of the flan case.
3. Microwave on a suitable plate or tray on HIGH for 3–5 minutes, turning the plate halfway through cooking if your oven does not have a turntable.
4. Allow a standing time of 5 minutes before serving hot; or serve cold.

Upside-down Pudding

Results from the microwave are excellent.

Serves 4–6

	Met.	Imp.
Butter	25g	1 oz
Brown sugar	25g	1 oz
Can of fruit, such as pineapple, apricot halves, peach slices, pear halves, cherries	411g	14½ oz
Butter or margarine	100g	4 oz
Caster sugar	75g	3 oz
Eggs, size 3, beaten	2	2
Self-raising flour	100g	4 oz
Milk		

Method

1. Melt the 25g/1 oz butter in a straight-sided dish on HIGH for about 30 seconds. Tilt the dish to spread the butter over its base.
2. Sprinkle the brown sugar over the butter and arrange the drained fruit in this.
3. Beat together the 100g/4 oz butter/margarine and caster sugar until light and fluffy. Gradually add the eggs,

beating well, then fold in the flour. Add sufficient milk to form a soft dropping consistency.

4. Spread the sponge mix evenly over the fruit.
5. Microwave, uncovered, on HIGH for 6–9 minutes, turning the pudding once or twice during cooking.
6. Allow a standing time of 10 minutes before turning out of the container.

10

CAKES, PASTRY AND BISCUITS

HANDY HINTS FOR CAKE-MAKING

Microwaved cakes rise well and their flavour is good. The texture will be slightly different from cakes cooked in a conventional oven with its dry, external heat, and of course, they will not brown or crisp. Once you have accepted this difference you will want to try your own recipes in the microwave.

Fat-free sponges of the whisked type are suitable for microwave cooking. But you must take care as they easily overcook.

Recipes which involve melting together ingredients such as fat, sugar and syrup are particularly suitable for microwave cooking.

Rich fruit cakes (including Christmas'cakes) can be cooked in the microwave. The results will be different each time but do not let this put you off. Cook them on DEFROST. A 20cm/ 8 in straight-sided, round cake takes 45 minutes – 1 hour on DEFROST. The top of the cake will appear slightly uncooked but a skewer inserted in the centre should come out clean after a 10 minute standing time. The cake can always be returned to the microwave for extra cooking.

The shape of a cake container is important (see page 13). Ring shapes are the most successful for any cake, followed by circles, squares and oblongs. The corners of oblongs and squares tend to cook more quickly than other areas and can be protected with a little foil – but check with your instruction book concerning the use of foil first.

Line containers with non-stick paper or greased greaseproof paper to assist with easy removal of cakes. Never flour the container or an unpalatable crust will form on the outside of the cake.

Half-fill the cooking container to allow the cake to rise. It will shrink back a little on removal from the oven.

Cakes evaporate more quickly in the microwave oven so, generally, about one quarter extra liquid is needed. When a recipe includes baking powder, try it out for the first time with about one quarter less baking powder. Microwaved cakes rise rapidly and too much raising agent will take them too high (and they will collapse when the microwave energy is switched off).

To decide which power level to use – check with a similar recipe in your instruction book. Generally, plain cakes are cooked on HIGH (though you may find better results are achieved on lower powers), while fruit cakes are cooked on LOW or DEFROST.

Cook one cake at a time. Cakes over 20cm/8 in diameter are not generally successful. Stand rich fruit cakes on a rack to encourage even cooking. To help a cake rise evenly turn it in its container, every couple of minutes if your oven does not have an automatic turntable. Do not be afraid to open the door briefly, the cake will rise again once you switch the power back on.

Cooking times will depend on the type and size of cake. The cake should be removed from the oven when it still looks slightly moist on its surface.

Small cakes should be arranged in a circle. If you put one in the middle it will cook much more slowly than the others.

Allow a standing time of 5–10 minutes before turning the cake out of its container.

Extra colouring can be added in the form of brown sugar, wholemeal flour, cocoa, chocolate, and so on. Sprinkle pale-looking cakes with a coating of icing sugar or add a tempting topping of icing, marzipan, a jam glaze on fruit and nuts, or toasted coconut or nuts.

Dried fruit can be plumped up in the microwave before adding it to a cake mixture. This helps to produce cakes which are beautifully moist. In a bowl, cover 225g/8 oz raisins, currants or sultanas with water, fruit juice or cold tea. Microwave, uncovered, on HIGH for 3 minutes. Cover the bowl and allow the fruit to stand for 5 minutes. Cool and drain to use in cake-making.

Cake mixes may be cooked in your microwave. Some brands produce better results than others so you will need to try them out.

Defrost cakes in the microwave. Place them on a sheet of absorbent paper and microwave on DEFROST:

1 small (fairy) cake or individual slice of cake takes 15- 30 seconds
2 small (fairy) cakes take 30 seconds
4 small (fairy) cakes take 1–2 minutes
A 20cm/8 in cake takes 2–3 minutes.

Allow a defrosting standing time of 2 minutes for small cakes and 5–10 minutes for large cakes.

Take care when defrosting cakes with a cream filling or decoration. The cream may melt before the cake defrosts. It is better to allow these to defrost naturally.

Additional tips

Soften sugar by placing it in a dish with a slice of lemon and heating on HIGH for 30 seconds – 1 minute.

Dry orange and lemon rinds in the microwave ready for use in cakes, see page 110.

Measure golden syrup easily – see page 112.

Clarify honey – see page 112.

Melt chocolate – see page 108.

Toast coconut – see page 108.

Blanch almonds by bringing about 300ml/½ pt water to the boil on HIGH. Add some almonds and microwave on HIGH for 2 minutes. Drain the almonds and when they are cool enough to handle, rub off their skins.

Toast nuts including almonds by one of these methods.
1. Spread blanched, skinned nuts (halved or chopped) on a plate and microwave, uncovered on HIGH until they turn golden brown. Stir the nuts or shake the plate frequently and remove nuts which have turned brown or they will tend to burn.
2. Place a small quantity of skinned, halved or chopped nuts in a small container with a small knob of butter. Microwave, uncovered, on HIGH until they reach the required colour. Stir or shake the nuts frequently to encourage even browning. Take care when handling the dish – it becomes very hot.

Dry breadcrumbs
Cut four slices of bread into small cubes and arrange them

on absorbent paper. Microwave on HIGH for about 4 minutes, checking and shaking them every minute, or until they are dry enough to crumble.

Toasted breadcrumbs
175g/6 oz breadcrumbs need about 50g/2 oz butter. Melt the butter on HIGH for about 1 minute. Stir in the breadcrumbs and coat them well with the butter. Microwave uncovered on HIGH for about 10 minutes or until golden brown. Stir often.

CAKE RECIPES

Date and Carrot Cake

I have included this recipe as it is a favourite of mine – the carrots give the cake a moist texture. See the note on page 112 for measuring golden syrup.

	Met.	*Imp.*
Butter or margarine	175g	6 oz
Light brown sugar	175g	6 oz
Golden syrup	6 x 15ml sp	6 tbsp
Self-raising flour	275g	10 oz
Mixed spice	2 x 5ml sp	2 tsp
Salt	pinch	pinch
Eggs, size 3, beaten	3	3
Carrots, grated	225g	8 oz
Dates, stoned and chopped	175g	6 oz

Method
1. Place the butter or margarine, sugar and syrup in a large container and microwave on HIGH for 2–3 minutes.
2. Stir in the flour, mixed spice, and salt.
3. Beat in the eggs then add the grated carrots and chopped dates.
4. Divide the mixture between two greased 18cm/7 in

containers. Lining the base with non-stick paper helps the cakes turn out easily.
5. Microwave *each* container, uncovered, for 6–8 minutes on HIGH.
6. Cool before turning the cakes out of their container.

Meringues

Meringue mixture for cooking in the microwave needs to be very stiff if it is to hold its shape. Use 275–350g/10–12 oz icing sugar to one egg white (size 3). This will make about 20 small meringues which can be sandwiched together with whipped cream. Beat together the egg white and icing sugar to make a firm paste. Divide into small balls. Arrange eight at a time in a circle on a plate or turntable covered with non-stick paper. Microwave uncovered on HIGH for 1½–2 minutes until risen and firm to the touch. They are cooked when they do not shrink on opening the oven door. Allow to cool.

Victoria Sandwich

This can be microwaved on HIGH or MEDIUM. The latter setting produces a lighter texture. You will probably wish to decorate the cake with icing sugar, icing etc. to cover its pale surface.

	Met.	Imp.
Butter or margarine	110g	4 oz
Caster sugar	110g	4 oz
Eggs, size 2	2	2
Self-raising flour, sifted	110g	4 oz
Milk		

Method A

1. Microwave the butter on HIGH for 5–10 seconds to soften it.
2. Cream the butter and sugar together until they are light and fluffy.
3. Gradually beat in the eggs.
4. Fold in the sifted flour, adding sufficient milk to make a soft consistency. (About 1 x 15ml sp/1 tbsp if cooking on MEDIUM, up to 3 x 15ml sp/3 tbsp if cooking on HIGH.)
5. Divide the mixture between two greased, lined (the base only) 18cm/7 in containers.
6. Microwave *each* container on MEDIUM for about 4 minutes, or on HIGH for about 3 minutes. Turn the container once or twice in those microwave ovens without turntables. The surface should still look slightly moist, while a skewer inserted in the centre comes out clean.
7. Allow a standing time of 10 minutes before turning each cake out of its container.

Method B

1. Soften the butter in the microwave on HIGH for 5–10 seconds.
2. Place all the ingredients in a bowl and mix thoroughly – an electric mixer is best for this.
3. Continue as 5, 6 and 7 in Method A.

Ring the changes: Make a *chocolate cake* by replacing 2 x 15ml sp/2 tbsp flour with the same quantity of cocoa or chocolate powder. Flavour the cake with orange or lemon rind and juice.

HANDY HINTS FOR MAKING PASTRY

Shortcrust pastry cooks well in the microwave – it is crisp and has a good flavour. It is better cooked without a filling. This can be added to the flan case later. Double crust pies cannot be microwaved since the base will not cook and the filling will overflow. Pastry containing sugar is not successful since the sugar tends to burn. Puff pastry is best cooked conventionally. Suet pastry cooks well so long as it is covered to retain maximum moisture.

Defrosting pastry dishes is successful. An empty pastry flan case need not be defrosted. It can be filled (and cooked) from frozen. Large flans, quiches and tarts from the freezer should be microwaved on DEFROST for about 5 minutes, depending on their filling, then allowed to stand for 5 minutes. If it is still icy, return it to the microwave for an extra 1–2 minutes before standing it again.

Large pies are difficult to defrost since the pastry defrosts before the filling and is liable to heat up while the filling is still frozen. Therefore microwave pies on DEFROST until the pastry is just warm to touch, then allow defrosting to continue naturally.

Reheating pastry dishes
Many pastry dishes which cannot be cooked successfully by microwaves will, in fact, reheat in the microwave with excellent results. Beware of over-heating though or the pastry will become soggy and spoil. Individual portions of flans, pies etc. need only about 1 minute on HIGH. Microwave them in the serving dish or on a sheet of absorbent paper.

Sausage rolls: 4 take 1–1½ minutes on HIGH depending on their size. One sausage roll takes about 15 seconds.

Cooked, filled *vol-au-vents* reheat well. Make their filling in the microwave too – see page 102 for hints on sauce-making.

PASTRY RECIPES

Shortcrust Pastry Case

Rolling the pastry out using wholemeal flour helps give an attractive colour to otherwise pale pastry. Do not add sugar to the mixture – it will burn. Use milk instead of water to mix the dough – this gives a better result.

1. Line a suitable flan dish with the pastry, prick the pastry case all over with a fork, particularly at the bend in the dish.
2. Cover the pastry base with two layers of absorbent kitchen paper to absorb the steam. Place an upturned plate or saucer on the paper.
3. Cook on HIGH for 2½–3 minutes, turning the dish every minute.
4. Stand for 5 minutes. Remove the plate and paper. The pastry should appear opaque.

Bakewell Tart

1. Prepare and microwave a shortcrust pastry case following the hints above. Allow it to cool.
2. Spread a layer of jam over the base of the flan case and top with a victoria sandwich mix flavoured with almond essence (recipe page 134).
3. Microwave, uncovered, for 5–6 minutes on HIGH. The surface will appear slightly moist but the sponge will feel firm to touch.
4. *Either* allow it to stand for 5 minutes before serving hot. *Or* cool the tart and top with thin icing and flaked almonds to disguise the pale top.

Quiche or Savoury Flan: Recipe page 61.

Scones

Sweet or savoury scones can be microwaved and are best cooked in a browning dish if you want the more traditional finish. Look for a recipe in the instruction book which comes with the browning dish.

HINTS FOR MAKING BISCUITS

Cookie-type biscuits are the most suitable for cooking by microwaves – six biscuits at a time on a sheet of non-stick or greaseproof paper. Best results are obtained when cooked on MEDIUM. Six take about 2–3 minutes. Stand for 5 minutes before lifting off the paper and cooling on a wire rack. Cooking on HIGH tends to produce rather dry, harder biscuits. Of course you will not achieve traditional golden colours, but biscuits can be sprinkled with chopped nuts or cherries before cooking or with icing sugar after cooking, or decorate them with chocolate (half-dipping gives attractive results) or icing.

BISCUIT RECIPES

Flapjacks

These will not be quite so crisp when cooked by microwaves. See page 112 for an easy way to measure golden syrup.

Makes 8 pieces

	Met.	Imp.
Golden syrup	3 x 15ml sp	3 tbsp
Sugar	100g	4 oz
Butter	100g	4 oz
Rolled oats	225g	8 oz
Egg, size 3, beaten	1	1

Baking powder	1 x 5ml sp	1 tsp
Salt	pinch	pinch

Method
1. Place the golden syrup, sugar and butter in a suitable container. Microwave on HIGH for 2-3 minutes or until the sugar has dissolved.
2. Stir in the rolled oats with the beaten egg, baking powder and salt.
3. Spread the mixture into a round, shallow container (18-20cm/7-8 in) lined with non-stick or greased greaseproof paper.
4. Microwave on HIGH for 4-6 minutes, turn the dish once or twice in those ovens without turntables.
5. Allow to stand for 5 minutes then mark into sections with a knife.
6. Allow the flapjacks to cool in the container before cutting them.

Shortbread

Makes 6-8 pieces

	Met.	Imp.
Butter	225g	8 oz
Caster sugar	100g	4 oz
Plain flour	275g	10 oz
Fine semolina	50g	2 oz

Method
1. Cream together the butter and sugar until they are light and fluffy.
2. Sieve the flour and semolina and fold these gently into the mixture. Knead the mixture lightly to form a dough.
3. Roll out or press the dough into a round 20cm/8 in container or onto a plate lined with greased greaseproof paper. If your oven has a turntable simply cover this with greased greaseproof paper and place the dough circle on it.

4. Prick the dough well with a fork and microwave uncovered on HIGH for 4–5 minutes.
5. Mark it into portions after 5 minutes' standing time, and sprinkle with caster sugar.
6. When cool, cut the shortbread into portions.

11

BREAD AND TEABREAD

BREAD
Rising, proving and cooking bread requires a microwave oven with variable power control.

Make up your usual bread mixture.

Rising:
1. Place the well-kneaded dough in a lightly oiled, large bowl. Turn the dough in the bowl to make sure it is coated with a fine layer of oil.
2. Cover the bowl loosely with non-stick paper, stand it in a shallow dish of hot water and microwave on LOW for 4 minutes for a large loaf or 2 minutes for a small loaf or rolls.
3. Allow the dough to stand for 15–20 minutes.
4. Repeat the process until the dough has doubled its size. Check regularly to see if the surface of the dough dries up. If you think it may be doing so, carefully turn the dough over in the bowl.
5. Knead the dough well and shape for proving.

Proving:
1. Place the shaped dough in a lightly oiled microwave loaf dish or other container.
2. Repeat the microwaving and standing processes 2–4 above (in a dish of hot water) until the dough has again doubled its size. Be patient – the bread must not start to cook.

Cooking:
1. Place the container on a cooking rack or upturned dish.
2. For a large loaf, microwave on MEDIUM for 6–7 minutes then on HIGH for 4–7 minutes; for a small loaf or rolls, microwave on MEDIUM for 3–4 minutes then on HIGH for 3–4 minutes. Turn the bread two or three times during cooking if your oven does not have a turntable. The bread is cooked when it springs back into shape when tested (all over) with the fingers.
3. Allow the bread to stand for 5 minutes then turn it out and cool on a wire rack.

HANDY HINTS FOR BREAD-MAKING
You may prefer to combine the use of the microwave with your conventional oven, speeding up the process by rising and proving in the microwave and cooking in the conventional oven to achieve the traditional crisp, brown finish.

Microwave-baked bread requires careful watching if it is not to over-cook at any stage. Practice, as usual, makes perfect.

The pale colour of microwave-cooked bread can be disguised by sprinkling with attractive toppings before cooking, such as cracked wheat, poppy seeds, sesame seeds and so on.

Microwave-baked rolls can be browned under the grill. Microwave-baked loaves can be put into a very hot, conventional oven for a few minutes to brown if liked.

Bread can be freshened in the microwave. Wrap it in kitchen paper and microwave on HIGH for up to 10 seconds.

Speed up the process considerably by using easy-bake yeast, which is stirred into the flour during mixing. The dough then only needs to rise once before cooking.

Defrost breads in the microwave. Light, open textures will defrost more quickly than heavier, closer textures. Place the bread on a sheet of absorbent paper and microwave on DEFROST for loaves; rolls can be defrosted on HIGH. As a general guide:

1 roll or slice takes 10–15 seconds on HIGH
2 rolls or slices take 15–20 seconds on HIGH
3 rolls or slices take 20–30 seconds on HIGH
4 rolls or slices take 25–35 seconds on HIGH.

Allow a defrosting-standing time of 1–2 minutes for rolls.

A small loaf takes 4–6 minutes on DEFROST
A large loaf takes 6–8 minutes on DEFROST.
Turn a large loaf over, halfway through defrosting.

Allow a defrosting-standing time of 5–10 minutes for a small loaf, and 10–15 minutes for a large loaf.

TEABREAD

Teabread is quick and easy to prepare with the microwave. Its cooked appearance is more moist than that cooked conventionally. For a moist texture use cooking oil instead of hard fat.

1. Simply mix together all the ingredients of your favourite recipe, using sufficient extra liquid to make a slack mixture.

2. Pour into a loaf dish lined with non-stick paper or greased greaseproof paper. A transparent loaf dish is useful – a reliable way of checking if the teabread is cooked is to look at its base for signs of unbaked mixture.

   You may find that the corners of a loaf shape over-cook. If so, check with your instruction book regarding the use of foil in your model. If it is allowed, shield the short ends with foil. Do not allow it to touch the oven walls.

3. Placing the dish on an upturned saucer helps even cooking. Cooking times will vary according to the

mixture, to the shape and size of your loaf dish, and to your oven. A good guide is to cook on MEDIUM for the first 8–9 minutes then switch to HIGH for the final 2–6 minutes. Alternatively, cook on HIGH for 8–12 minutes.

4. Allow to stand for 5 minutes then test the centre of the cake with a cocktail stick or skewer. If it comes out clean the teabread is cooked. If not, microwave on HIGH for another minute then stand again.

5. Cool on a wire rack.

Date and Walnut Loaf

	Met.	Imp.
Dates, stoned and chopped	175g	6 oz
Walnuts, chopped	50g	2 oz
Sugar	175g	6 oz
Plain flour	175g	6 oz
Bicarbonate of soda	1 x 5ml sp	1 tsp
Salt	1 x 5ml sp	1 tsp
Cooking oil	60ml	4 tbsp
Egg, size 2 or 3, beaten	1	1
Grated rind of orange or lemon	1	1
Milk		

Method
1. Mix together all the ingredients, adding sufficient milk to make a slack mixture.
2. Follow steps 2–5 of the Teabread recipe above.

12

PRESERVES AND SWEETS

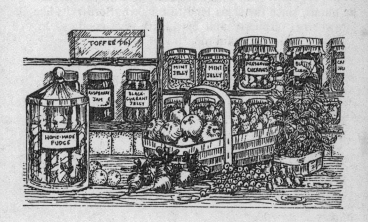

HINTS FOR MAKING PRESERVES

Jams, marmalades and chutneys can be made in the microwave oven, and both colour and flavour are good. They do not burn on the cooking container and generally need far less attention than preserves prepared conventionally on the hob. Small quantities are particularly suitable for cooking in the microwave. Large quantities are more successfully cooked conventionally (over 1.25kg/ 2½ lb).

Use a container which is two to three times as large as the quantity of preserve. It must have plenty of room to boil up. Always use a container which is suitable for high temperature cooking. Sugar mixtures become very hot. The container will get hot too, so use oven gloves.

Use a sugar thermometer but never leave it in the microwave oven when it is switched on – unless it is specifically designed for use in the microwave.

Microwaved marmalade will not have such tender peel. Jellies are better than jams when using fruit with skins, such as plums, since the skins tend to toughen. Soft-fruits like strawberry, raspberry and blackberry give good results. Lemon curd is successful too.

Always check with the instruction/recipe book for your model for advice on cooking times and power levels.

When converting your own recipes for jams, jellies and chutneys, use about half the amount of water.

RECIPES FOR PRESERVES

Raspberry Jam
Makes about 700g/1½ lb

	Met.	Imp.
Raspberries, washed and drained	450g	1 lb
Water	1 x 15ml sp	1 tbsp
Caster sugar	450g	1 lb

Method
1. Put the raspberries and water into a large, deep container.
2. Cook on HIGH, stirring once or twice, until the fruit is just cooked (4–5 minutes).
3. Add the caster sugar and stir until it dissolves.
4. Microwave, uncovered, on HIGH stirring every minute or so, until setting point is reached, about 10–12 minutes.
5. Cool, pot and label the jam.

Redcurrant Jelly

	Met.	Imp.
Redcurrants, washed and drained	900 g	2 lb
Water	200 ml	⅓ pt
Caster sugar: to each 550ml/1 pt juice	450 g	1 lb

Method

1. Place the redcurrants and the water in a large, deep container.
2. Microwave on HIGH, stirring occasionally until the fruit boils and turns to a rough purée.
3. Allow the mixture to cool before tipping it into a fine nylon sieve, muslin or a jelly bag. Allow the juice to strain through. Do not press the fruit through or the jelly will be cloudy.
4. Measure the liquid and add 450g/1 lb caster sugar to each 550ml/1 pt juice.
5. Microwave on HIGH, stirring occasionally, until the sugar dissolves.
6. Continue to cook on HIGH until setting point is reached.
7. Cool, pot and label the jelly.

Apple Jelly

	Met.	Imp.
Cooking or crab apples, diced with the peel and core left on	900 g	2 lb
Water	400 ml	¾ pt
Caster Sugar: to each 550ml/1 pt juice	450 g	1 lb

Method

Follow steps 1–7 as for Redcurrant Jelly.

Mint Jelly

Makes about 900g/2 lb

	Met.	Imp.
Mint, whole leaves	40g	1½ oz
Caster sugar	450g	1 lb
Vinegar	250ml	½ pt
Certo	225ml	slightly less than ½ pt
Green food colouring		
Mint, chopped	15g	½ oz

Method

1. Mix together the mint leaves, sugar and vinegar in a large, deep container.
2. Microwave on HIGH for 8–10 minutes or until the sugar dissolves.
3. Remove the mint and boil the remaining mixture on HIGH for about 1 minute.
4. Strain the mixture through a fine nylon sieve, muslin or a jelly bag.
5. Stir in the Certo and a little green food colouring.
6. Microwave on HIGH for 4–5 minutes, stirring once or twice, then stir in the chopped mint.
7. Cool, pot and label the jelly.

Beetroot and Apple Chutney

Makes about 1.5kg/3 lb

	Met.	Imp.
Beetroot	450g	1 lb
Water	4 x 15ml sp	4 tbsp
Cooking apples, peeled, cored and diced	450g	1 lb
Onions, chopped finely	225g	8 oz
Vinegar	400ml	¾ pt
Ground cummin	½ x 5ml sp	½ tsp

| Celery salt | ½ x 5ml sp | ½ tsp |
| Salt | ½ x 5ml sp | ½ tsp |

Method
1. Place the washed (unpeeled) beetroot into a suitable container with the water. Cover and cook on HIGH for 7–8 minutes or until the beetroot is tender. Cool, remove the skin and chop the beetroot finely.
2. Place the apples, onion, vinegar, spices and salt into a large, deep container. Cover and cook on HIGH until the onion is soft, about 5 minutes.
3. Stir in the beetroot, cover and microwave on HIGH for about 10 minutes. Uncover and microwave on HIGH until the mixture has thickened. Stir once or twice during cooking.
4. Cool, pot and label the chutney.

HINTS FOR MAKING SWEETS
Sweets, toffee and fudge are easy to make with the microwave. They do not stick or burn and the results are good. Use the microwave to melt chocolate to coat nuts and fruits and to make truffles.

Generally use a little less liquid since there is less evaporation in the microwave.

Use a container which is 2–3 times the size of the amount of sweet mixture. It may boil up dramatically. Sugar mixtures reach very high temperatures so make sure that you choose a container which is suitable.

Use oven gloves – the container becomes hot.

Use a sugar thermometer, but never leave it in the mixture while the microwave energy is switched on unless it is a special microwave thermometer.

Check the temperature frequently to avoid over-cooking.

Do not cover the container when making sweets.

RECIPES FOR SWEETS

Fudge

Makes about 450g/1 lb
See page 112 for easy measuring of golden syrup.

	Met.	*Imp.*
Caster sugar	450g	1 lb
Golden syrup	2–3 x 15ml sp	2–3 tbsp
Butter	50g	2 oz
Orange juice	2 x 15ml sp	2 tbsp
Condensed milk, full cream	7 x 15ml sp	7 tbsp

Method
1. Put all the ingredients into a large, deep container.
2. Cook, uncovered, on HIGH for 7–8 minutes, or until it reaches setting point. Drop a little into cold water – it should set. If using a thermometer the mixture should reach 115°C/238°F.
3. Beat the mixture, then pour it into a lightly greased square tin.
4. Cut into squares when cold.

Toffee

Makes 550g/1¼ lb
See page 112 for easy measuring of golden syrup.

	Met.	*Imp.*
Golden syrup	225g	8 oz
Granulated sugar	225g	8 oz
Butter	100g	4 oz

Method
1. Place all the ingredients in a large, deep container.
2. Microwave on HIGH for 6–7 minutes, stirring frequently,

until a little dropped in a cup of cold water sets. If using a thermometer it should reach 138°C/280°F.
3. Pour the toffee into a lightly greased, square tin.
4. Cut into squares just before it is completely set.

INDEX

Words in italics refer to actual recipes.